Gathering Force

DIY Culture   Radical action for those tired of waiting

Elaine Brass and Sophie Poklewski Koziell

Edited by Denise Searle

Writers	Elaine Brass
	Sophie Poklewski Koziell
Editor	Denise Searle
Cover photograph	Alex MacNaughton
	Claremont Rd, M11, July 1994
Photography	Sarah Chesworth
	Nick Cobbing
	David Hoffman
	Alan Lodge
	Alex MacNaughton
	Steve Mayes
	Adrian Short
	Alec Smart
	Andrew Testa
Illustration	Paul Render
Design	Jo Shackleton
Print	BPC Wheatons Ltd, Exeter
	Printed on 100% recycled paper
Image Setting	FE Burmans Ltd, London
c 1997	Sophie Poklewski Koziell
	Elaine Brass

ISBN 1899419012 1st Edition

British Library Cataloguing in Publication Data.
A catalogue record for this book is available
from the British Library.

Published 1997 by The Big Issue Writers,
Fleet House,
57-61 Clerkenwell Road,
London EC1M 5NP.
Tel 0171 418 0418

Thanks to Battlebridge Centre, The Big Issue, Dr Tony Hare,
Nick Harris, Manchester Museum of Labour
History, Manchester Central Library, Media Natura,
Stephen Murphy, Network for Social Change, the
Ploughshares Support Network, Dylan Tanner
and the many other generous people who gave
us their time, help and support.

Contents

preface

In the last five years there has been a noticeable increase in direct action and "alternative lifestyles" in Britain. This book describes this so-called "DIY Culture" and attempts to give a voice to the people who are "Doing It Themselves". We travelled around the UK to meet and interview more than 100 individuals directly involved in a variety of aspects of DIY: long-time campaigners, young activists, people who have opted out of mainstream society, specialist journalists, political commentators and those in power. These interviews are set against our attempt to define and assess DIY Culture, and to give it some kind of historical perspective. We have drawn on the mass of literature DIY Culture has stimulated, both from the conventional press and the alternative media this new movement has generated. The text is interspersed with dramatic images from some of the most remarkable photographers in this country, who have tirelessly documented all the various strands of DIY Culture.

Elaine Brass
Sophie Poklewski Koziell
July 1997

Forward by A John Bird

The Big Issue was created in the spirit of the Do It Yourself (DIY) philosophy. It was formed in opposition to a lot of people who said: "Who are you to start The Big Issue when you don't have a degree in social anthropology? Who are you to start a publication when there are publications closing all the time? Who are you to work with homeless people who have such severe social problems that you need all sorts of medical and social training to work with them?" We said: "Well, we don't really give a damn what people are saying, we're just going to get on with it." And we have proved that outside the mainstream you can do things that are practical, credible and that improve the lives of many, many individuals.

The Big Issue has taken up the problems of people who, for all sorts of reasons, don't accept the political, social and economic patterns of the day and therefore try to find solutions that reflect their desire to take control of their own lives. We have published this book because we recognise DIY Culture as a tangible alternative to the rat race, the alienation and all the other things that have developed in modern society. One of the most refreshing sides of DIY Culture – and its strength – is that the people within it don't claim that there is only one alternative to the mainstream or that there is only one way to be involved in self-help.

This book is many things: it is informative; it shows people involved in practical solutions; it shows support for people who are often disregarded and derided; and it is a rallying call to encourage people to realise that they can do things in alternative ways. Above all, it is a celebration of the many, many people who have rescued themselves from the kind of cynicism and empty thoughtlessness that came out of the 18 years of Conservative rule.

The fact that this new administration may not be so sinister and cynical as the previous government does not in any way guarantee that people involved in DIY Culture will receive more money or social support. In fact any community or grassroots manifestation can't really fit in neatly with those in power because they have different aims and purposes. What I would like to hope is that this new government will leave DIY Culture to develop by itself, to remain independent and self-functioning as an alternative to mass production and mass pollution.

Introduction

The Peterloo Massacre 1819
Manchester Central Library, Local Studies Unit

Conscience and Necessity

"It is all about people regaining their dignities and their own particular truths, because what is out there at this juncture is next to zero."

Ronnie The Solidarity Centre, a community project in Glasgow

The 1990s will be remembered as the decade in which Britain became gripped by a new aggressive environmentalism. Suddenly people who have never taken a political stance before are finding their voices and demonstrating their opposition to the actions of the Government or industry, and generally demanding their rights.

At first glance, it seemed as if we had suddenly been transported into the middle of a new protest culture. Some Government ministers and the right-wing press have tried to dismiss the action as being stirred up by a minority of extremists engaged in a kind of eco-war. But a closer look reveals these actions to be the radical face of something that goes much deeper: a relatively small number of individuals are vocalising and acting upon the frustration and anxieties that run right through society. People who call themselves apolitical, who aren't interested in or aligned to any political party, many of whom don't even vote, are being political in other ways.

The protests are very diverse and many of the people who turn out on the picket lines to try to stop the live exports of sheep and veal calves probably wouldn't dream of camping out in tree houses to prevent woodland being destroyed by yet another bypass. However strong bonds have been formed at these protests between people of different generations and with contrasting backgrounds, and these have led to considerable cross support in subsequent struggles. There is a common link between the animal lovers and the anti-roads activists (and even with those campaigning for the right to hold raves and against the Criminal Justice Act): many of them have tried conventional channels for change, but have got so fed up with the lack of response that they have decided to take matters into their own hands.

And it's not just a question of having to wait too long for things to get better; increasing numbers of people are coming to the conclusion that their needs will never be addressed by those in power. They feel that public institutions and the Government are too busy trying to compete in the global free market economy to actually listen to the needs and ideas of the individuals and communities that make up this nation. We now have the most centralised system of government since before the Second World War, accompanied by a weakening of local authorities, trade unions, legal aid and other sources of power and change that have traditionally been accessible to ordinary people. One third of all public expenditure is now spent by unelected quangos (Quasi Non Governmental Organisations) and gas, water, electricity and many other essential public services have been privatised.

Therefore those involved in Do It Yourself Culture are taking responsibility for and control over their own lives. As Peter Hope, a spokesperson for the disabled people's Direct Action Network, puts it: "You can advocate for years, you can write to MPs, you can protest about lots of things, but you have to learn to be socially disobedient and say 'well, actually this is an issue that affects my whole life'. It is about being visible and it is about being strong."

Activists say DIY Culture means making small changes individually and locally, rather than hanging about waiting for one big global remedy for all social and environmental ills. It is about standing up for the things they believe in and about taking responsibility for themselves, the environment and the community. They feel they should be looking after themselves and others, not just hoping that somebody else will do it. Most of all, they believe they can make a difference.

"The whole business of DIY Culture is that you get together and you say 'This an issue that affects us, the people in this room, and we want to do something about it'," says George Monbiot, one of the founders of The Land Is Ours land rights movement and a researcher at the Centre for Environmental Policy and Understanding at Green College, Oxford. "We are not MPs, we are not elected representatives – the popular mandate is ourselves."

Mainstream media reports portray DIY Culture as being based mainly on environmental and animal rights campaigns but, when you talk to those involved, you see that these so-called "single" issues are just a focus and starting point for debate and action on a wider scale. DIY Culture encompasses far more: homelessness, quality of life, unemployment, economic alternatives, land rights, civil rights. However the status of the environment is seen as an indicator that all else is well in society; when it is seen to be continually and unapologetically destroyed, the "environment" becomes the stimulus for action.

"The notion of DIY being 'single issue' is rapidly being dispelled," reckons John Vidal, environment editor, of The Guardian. "It is the same as what happened in Eastern Europe – which is that the pro-democracy movements started off as environmental campaigns which tended to attract people who were very idealistic, but then they moved on very quickly and people realised that it was all tied in with social issues." Added to that in the UK was the Criminal Justice and Public Order Act 1994 which did a good job of uniting people with a wide range of concerns: from ramblers to travellers, trade unionists to squatters.

DIY Culture isn't confined to any class, area or issue and it is much more than simple politics: most DIYers live and breathe their causes. They want direct action and take it. They are much more impatient than some past generations of political activists who put up with all the layers and the time lag that exist between going to a meeting or march and any positive result that might be achieved. The movement is bigger than the sum of its parts; it is a kind of common sense.

Seen from the outside, DIY Culture can seem to be about dreadlocks, juggling, living up trees and tribes with strange names. But it is more than that. It is also about trying to bypass institutions and monolithic structures to do light-hearted, individualistic empowering. This can mean anything

Anti Criminal Justice Act
Westminster, November 1994
Protest by members of the
No M11 Link Campaign.

Photo: Nick Cobbing

CONVICTED OF FELONY,
And Transported for SEVEN YEARS

COUNTY OF DORSET.
Dorchester Division.

February 22d, 1834.

C. B. WOLLASTON,
JAMES FRAMPTON,
WILLIAM ENGLAND,
THOS. DADE,
JNO. MORTON COLSON.

HENRY FRAMPTON,
RICHD. TUCKER STEWARD,
WILLIAM R. CHURCHILL,
AUGUSTUS FOSTER.

G. CLARK, PRINTER, CORNHILL, DORCHESTER.

THE   MEN   CONCERNED

Tolpuddle Martyrs 1834
Six farm labourers from the Dorset village of Tolpuddle deported to Australia
for seven years for organising themselves into a union.

Photo: Manchester Museum of Labour History

from writing a letter to standing in front of a bulldozer. The latter – non-violent direct action (NVDA) – is the more visible side of DIY Culture and one strongly associated with it.

Yet DIY Culture is not just a series of short-term actions. It is equally about the continuous, quiet, background organisation, the communication networks, the sharing of knowledge and experiences, the gathering of resources, the steady building of working alternatives. "It consists of a lot of little local groups, but if you look at the whole there is an evolving atmosphere in the underground of taking power into your own hands and doing something for yourself and your community," explains Steve Thackeray, a member of the Leeds grouping of the radical environmental network Earth First!

"There is a very different culture of politics growing up," says Geoff Mulgan, director of the left-wing think tank Demos. "But it is also much wider than that. It is about people wanting to take responsibility for their own lifestyles and realising that how they live – in terms of their own health or what they consume – is actually a political action. It's a realisation that individual actions influence the overall fabric of society and how it works."

Jamie Hartzell, director of the Small World environmental media group, sees it in a slightly different way: "In DIY Culture, the lifestyle comes before politics. A percentage of the people are highly political: the rest are subscribing to the politics as part of the lifestyle."

Regardless of what comes first – the politics or the lifestyle – one common strand is clear: a strong disillusionment with all the mainstream political parties and with the whole political, social and economic system, including national and local institutions, and big commercial interests. It is a sense of disappointment with democracy as it is practised in Britain today.

"There ought to be a series of mechanical links from voter to party to Parliament to state," says Andrew Marr, editor of The Independent and author of Ruling Britannia. "The voter tugs and the thing works and something happens at the level of the state. But every one of those single links has been allowed to decay… the voting system is no longer adequate to reflect the variety of things that we want. We are offered a black and white choice with the attitude that if you don't like it you can forget it."

Some politicians, like Labour's National Heritage Secretary Chris Smith, accept that the people involved in politics sometimes don't really want to listen. "Parliament and Government tend to be a bit out of touch with a lot of thinking and modes of speech that – particularly young – people are using," he admits. "There are certain problems with communication where there is no shared language, no shared assumptions and no culture."

This is partly to do with the generation gap: before the May 1997 general election the average age of Conservative MPs was 64 and of Labour 47 and this has not altered much. However, the problem goes much deeper. There is bound to be a significant difference in outlook and terminology between the voted-in and the voter; and this seems to have grown over recent years.

To some extent, this is deliberate, thinks Smith: "Parts of the establishment do not want to know about grassroots concerns. Not only are they being very blinkered and prejudiced to take that attitude, but I also think that they are being foolish. The establishment has been at its most successful when it has absorbed ideas and demands that have come from the outside; votes for women being a classic example. Unless you have that healthy flow of demands coming through, the political system will just fossilise."

Chris Rose, Campaigns Director of the environmental lobby group Greenpeace holds a similar view. "The Government treats a lot of people's concerns as technical issues to be dealt with and disposed of and contained by groups of scientists, or committees that you can never reach," he says. "Take animal testing, Brent Spar and electro-magnetic radiation. These are all treated as issues that a committee of people deals with and you don't have any say in it."

Yet Greenpeace is now a huge organisation in its own right and has relatively good access to those in power. At grassroots level, you find even more disillusionment: "Basically, politicians don't represent me – they just keep me down," complains Alan Lodge, a photographer and chairperson of Friends, Families and Travellers. "I would like to feel represented because I understand that we are not all anarchistic, we do need some kind of representation of what people think. So we have to do something about it."

Many of those involved in DIY Culture haven't completely lost faith in the political process. They are sceptical, but will use existing structures where appropriate. "Where campaigns have been most successful is where they have done everything: used their local councils, politicians, held stunts, been pro-active – worked both within the system as well as outside it," says Emma Must, the award-winning coordinator of the anti-roads group Alarm UK.

Not everyone wants to or can take direct action. Some sink into apathy, others get on with carving out a career to buy their way out of the destruction being wreaked on the countryside and to Britain's social services, health care and education systems. If you live in a "nice" area with the money for private medical insurance and school fees, maybe you can anaesthetise yourself to what's going on around you. But growing numbers of people don't have that option.

"There have always been people who have no money," says Jim Paton of the Advisory Service for Squatters. "But now there are a whole lot more who were comfortable and felt secure and now don't."

Steve Platt, former editor of New Statesman and Society reckons a major factor is unemployment, which is in reality far higher than the official figures once you discard the training schemes and various tactics to reduce the number of people entitled to claim benefit bought in by the Conservatives between 1979 and 1997. "It has meant that there is a greater number of people looking to do what they can for themselves," he says. "There is a sense of 'if the system such as it is can't supply us with a decent job, decent house, decent life and so on, then I am going to go out and do it for myself and have fun while I am doing it'."

This is where the positive side of DIY Culture can be seen to be improving the quality of people's lives through local exchange trading schemes (LETS), community banking, free parties and creating community centres from vacant buildings.

Liberal Democrat MP Simon Hughes applauds this kind of work: "In this country there has been very high unemployment and to be honest it is as good and acceptable a lifestyle to be living on very little income but achieving political objectives as seeking conventional employment – because there probably isn't any."

London, High Court, October 1908
Suffragettes watch as Christabel
Pankhurst conducts their defence

Photo: Manchester Museum of
Labour History

**Greenham Common Eviction,
April 1984**
Women's peace camp at the
gates of the Greenham Common
United States nuclear missile
base in Berkshire. The land which
housed the camp is owned by
the Department of Transport
which wanted it to make way
for a road-widening scheme.

Photo: Manchester Museum of
Labour History

DIY Culture may be a product of the 1990s but its roots are clearly in the long and honourable tradition of direct action in Britain. This people's history can be traced back to at least 1381, the date of the Peasants' Revolt against the unpopular first-poll tax, and has echoes through the intervening years, including the Levellers and Diggers in the 1640s with their demands for democracy and land rights. The rock group The Levellers, whose songs are usually a part of any DIY festival, demonstrate that many of today's activists are only too aware of their common ancestry.

The tradition of grassroots movements continued through the next two centuries with the bread riots and the protests against the enclosures of common land in the late 1700s; and the demonstrations against the Poor Law of 1834. In this century DIY action has included the Suffragettes' campaign for votes for women; the mass trespasses of Kinder Scout in the 1930s to win the right of public access to the Peak District and which led to the formation of the Ramblers Association; and the women's camps at Greenham Common air base in the 1980s to protest against nuclear weapons. These activities are as diverse as the 1990s' DIY Culture, and they demonstrate that if ordinary people have ever wanted something from those in economic or political power – be they Government ministers, landowners or factory bosses – they have always had to win it themselves.

"DIY Culture has always been an intrinsic part of British counter culture. Look back at any era, that is in essence how things have changed in this country," says Camilla Berens, former spokesperson for the Freedom Network (the anti-Criminal Justice Act coalition) and editor of POD magazine. "People have realised that the public and the politicians have grown too far apart. So they start to create their own systems."

Looking back through the ages, you discover amazing, often intentional, parallels with different aspects of today's DIY Culture. Take the Diggers, who created a commune in 1649 at St George's Hill in Surrey by invading barren heath claimed by a local landowner to graze cattle. Nine volunteers began by digging and manuring the land. Others joined them and they erected wooden huts for the first families, eventually the number there reached 100. They established an egalitarian community in which everyone shared the work, good times,

harvests and misfortunes. The commune withstood three months of repeated attacks on their crops and houses by soldiers and the local landowners' mobs before moving to a nearby piece of unenclosed common land from which they were evicted some months later. Fast forward nearly 350 years… in 1996 we had the five-month occupation of a development site in Wandsworth, south London, owned by the Guinness brewing company and left vacant for seven years. The 100 or so "eco-villagers" led by The Land Is Ours campaign, built homes, established communal areas, grew crops on the site, and established links with the local community – until they were evicted by 250 police in riot gear.

Or take the often misrepresented Luddites who attempted to defend the livelihoods of their communities between the years 1811 and 1813 against the onslaught of "progress" in the form of industrialisation of textile production. This industrial revolution enabled the employers to do away with skilled weavers and slash wages to starvation levels, producing a dramatic increase in child labour. Today people try to safeguard their communities from "progress" in a variety of ways. The protesters who have tried to stop new roads decimating parts of east London, Devon, Berkshire, Glasgow and numerous other places. Or the mining communities who fought for their survival in the face of sweeping and unnecessary pit closures, just so the electricity industry could import cheaper coal and gas from abroad. Or the Merseyside Dockers on strike for over a year in a battle against the introduction of casual labour schemes which will drive down wages, increase working hours, decrease job security and take away pension and sickness benefits.

The brutal ways DIYers have often been dealt with in recent times has shocked many people, including those middle-Englanders who had hitherto great faith in British law and order. The images of police roughly shoving elderly people out of the way of veal lorries and of tree houses being demolished with their occupants still in them will stay with us for a long time. However, we shouldn't be surprised: the British state has never taken kindly to grassroots opposition and has often retaliated with harsh new laws and tough tactics. In the mid-1700s there was a huge increase in hangings to punish crimes against property, such as tearing down fences that enclose common land and destroying the silk looms of exploitative employers.

In the 1990s we witnessed the jailing of activists for trying to sabotage the construction equipment of companies building major road schemes through environmentally-sensitive areas.

The Luddites' campaign of smashing the weaving frames of employers who cut workers' wages led to a new law which made frame-breaking a capital offence. Dozens of Luddites were hanged as a result. And how did a recent British Government deal with the strikes by trade unionists in the 1980s against the introduction of new technology in the printing industry and job losses in the coal mines? By sending in special squads of police to arrest strikers; laying siege to many mining villages; and by severe anti-union and public order legislation which still restricts picketing and public gatherings today.

Back in 1819, several thousand men, women and children who attended a peaceful anti-Government demonstration at Peterloo in Manchester were attacked by sabre-wielding troops and local businessmen on horseback. Eleven were killed and at least 500 were seriously injured. Again, flash to modern times and we're in Hyde Park in 1994 when a large but good-natured protest against the Criminal Justice Bill (before it became law) was scattered by mounted police. Or whizz to Stonehenge in 1986 where a group of travellers tried to celebrate the summer solstice but were set upon by riot police and driven off the land. Several of the travellers' vans (their homes) were destroyed and they were vilified in the right-wing newspapers.

Opposition to what are seen as unjust laws and regulations, or the oppressive or corrupt ways the authorities implement them, has frequently been the basis for popular protest. Ordinary people often feel a moral right to disobey laws and practices they regard as unfair, and to agitate for them to be scrapped. As Criminalising Diversity and Dissent, a report by the civil rights pressure group Liberty puts it: "Public support for Non-Violent Direct Action continues to grow. A Gallup poll reported in the Daily Telegraph showed that 68 per cent of people believe that there are times when protesters are justified in breaking the law, suggesting that there is a growing disillusionment with the response of politicians and governments to public opinion… The belief that it is sometimes right to break the law as a protest has spread from the traditionally more anarchic classes – to embrace all sections of opinion including those who used to know better."

This is not new. In the late eighteenth century, the country was gripped by food riots as hungry people challenged the profiteering of landowners – who were engaged in some early free-market economics – by taking food for themselves. It was like a forerunner of ethical shoplifting. In Honiton, Devon, in 1766, lace makers seized corn being held back by local farmers to force up the price, took it to market, sold it and returned the money and sacks to the farmers. In the "Great Cheese Riot" in Nottingham in 1764, whole cheeses were taken and rolled down the street. Meanwhile, in Halifax, merchants were forced to lower the price of oats and wheat so that ordinary people could afford them.

The Peasants' Revolt, mentioned above, in which a rebel band thousands strong captured the Tower of London and wrung concessions out of King Richard II, was prompted by the imposition of high taxes (known as the poll tax) on the poor, and the greed of the church authorities who did the collecting. More than 600 years later, opposition to another poll tax, which also hit the poorest people in society hardest, led to one of the biggest waves of civil disobedience in recent times. The courts became clogged with people being prosecuted because they refused to pay the unfair tax and a huge demonstration against it in London's Trafalgar Square in March 1990 became infamous for the way mounted police attacked the largely peaceful crowd. The good news was that the poll tax was scrapped as a result and the widespread opposition to it contributed to Margaret Thatcher's increasing unpopularity and her eventual ousting as Prime Minister and leader of the Conservative Party. The bad news was that the Trafalgar Square demonstration led the Tories to introduce one of their most stringent laws against public protests – the 1994 Criminal Justice Act – bound up with heavy new penalties targeted at a wide range of groups including squatters, hunt saboteurs, travellers and ravers.

Popular action has often paved the way for positive changes. When the Tolpuddle Martyrs – six Dorset farm labourers who tried in 1834 to form a trade union to improve their low wages – were deported, 800,000 people signed a petition to have the sentence annulled. It was. The men were given free passages back to the UK and the way was paved for legalising trade unions. Then there was George Lansbury and his fellow councillors in Poplar, east London who were sent to prison

Poll Tax Riots, London, March 1990

Photo: David Hoffman

early this century for refusing to set the level of council rates. They insisted that local residents, who were among the poorest in London, could not afford to foot the bill for the services they needed. Their case eventually established the practice of providing central funds to help socially-deprived areas (although this has been eroded over recent years by restrictions on local authority spending and cuts in central subsidies).

In fact, many of the basic services and rights that we now take for granted – such as health care, state education, social housing, redistribution of wealth via taxes and the right to vote – were achieved after hard-fought battles at grassroots level. Often these battles were supported by left-wing and liberal intellectuals whose writing and pronouncements helped increase pressure on the government of the day. Now, as these services are being eroded by spending cuts and the Conservative Government's philosophy of shifting more aspects of public life into private hands, people are once again having to use self-help to satisfy their own basic needs and those of the wider community.

"Even in Dickens time the amount of social activity, particularly by men, was tremendous. They were forever having dinners to raise money for an orphanage, a new sewer or to set up a school board," says The Independent's Andrew Marr. "There was a continuous bubble and ferment of little groups setting up – friendly societies and so on. It may be that in the middle of this century the sheer size of the state and the fact that we had this welfare which was going to do it all for us, actually subdued the other social activity. What we are seeing at the moment may be the slow return to what was there before – the norm."

Some commentators say that the nearest equivalent to today's DIY Culture is the protests of the late 1960s which hinged on the student demonstrations in 1968 in Britain, France, the United States and several other countries. "I grew up in the Sixties and one of the great things about that generation is that not only was there a flowering of culture but also there was an incredible sense of hope in the future and the acknowledgment that you could change the world through democratic actions," says Labour's Chris Smith. "That was what led people to demonstrate and protest and get involved in political parties. Everybody assumed that there was a possibility of change and that you as an individual could take part and make that change happen." One of the main similarities is the self confidence that both generations have, says Hilary Wainwright, editor of Red Pepper magazine and a long-time researcher into social movements. "In 1968 we were protesting that the universities were too authoritarian or that courses were boring. People didn't start by talking to their MP or writing to The Times, but went in for direct action such as occupying the buildings.

"There was a frustration with formal political structures which were seen as morally decadent. We had a certainty that it was right to take action ourselves. On the whole there was a concern for democracy and mass action involving as many parts of society as possible, which is where there are particularly strong parallels with the DIYers."

Wainwright reckons the main difference was that the late 1960s and early 1970s were more ideological than today's DIY Culture. "There was a regeneration of Marxism going on at the time in an attempt to understand things like the Vietnam War and the failures of social democracy," she explains. "The movements were enthused by heavy intellectual and ideological debate. The present movement is not totally unideological, but it is more eclectic and has an aversion to 'isms'. If there is a political influence it's anarchism rather than Marxism."

Whatley Quarry, December 1995
Lined up for action

Photo: Alec Smart

She admits that the 1960s activists were more privileged than now. Most were students on adequate grants or, if they were unemployed, there were decent dole payments. "Now, relatively few DIYers are in higher education and even if they are they need to take on part-time work in McDonald's or Burger King to supplement the meagre grants. The culture is driven by necessity."

Most DIYers would agree with this. However, many reject direct comparisons with the Sixties. They accept the historical connections but believe that DIY Culture is unique; that it hasn't happened before in quite the same way – that it is a sign of our times.

"The big difference with the sixties and now is that the hippies were mostly well-brought-up, white, middle class from educated backgrounds," says Nick Saunders, author of E for Ecstasy and founder of Neals Yard wholefoods and therapy centre in London's Covent Garden. "In comparison, this whole new generation is very broad-based; it seems to be the most culturally-mixed movement that there has been, and it is very unpretentious."

Bronisław Szerszynski, a lecturer at the Centre for Environmental Change at Lancaster University, sees the difference as a spiritual one. "People have a sense of themselves, a sort of private inner self, which they want to realise. It is a kind of individualism, but it is not just a consumerist individualism, it is a kind of potentially expressive individualism. Knowing who you are and doing your thing has become a slogan for the rest of the 20th Century. Through this very individualistic sense of choosing, people are not only changing their own lives, but are also discovering a sense of connectedness with other people."

Or, put more simply by Adrian Harris of the Dragon Environmental Network: "We learnt a hell of a lot from the Sixties – we've learnt what went wrong. Its roots weren't very deep, it was a very idealistic rebellion. There has to be a lot more grounding and that is what we have got now."

The other major difference is that in the Sixties, grassroots activists believed that a Labour government under Prime Minister Harold Wilson would mean real improvements in Britain. Many student radicals actually campaigned for a Labour victory in the 1964 general election. It's hard to see that happening now. More than one third of people aged between 18 and 25 didn't vote in 1992 or 1997: that's 2.5 million people. This was partly because some young people didn't register to vote in an attempt to avoid the poll tax, but commentators say it indicates a general trend. New Labour, with its authoritarian leanings, ecological laissez faire and preoccupation with crime and the concerns of middle England, failed to entice many of today's DIYers into the polling booths.

Some of the '68 energy continued into the 1970s with activities like the peace movement and the struggle for women's rights, with high-profile direct action such as disrupting the Miss World competition. Some Sixties activists began the long march into the Labour Party and are holding the fort as councillors or as the small band of left-wing MPs. Others went into academia; most gave up. The key question is: will the dynamism, inventiveness and passion of today's DIY Culture survive? The activists and their supporters think it will – in one form or another.

March on St George's Hill, April 1995
Part of The Land is Ours campaign

Photo: Nick Cobbing

"One of the problems of the last 20 years is that the Seventies and Eighties have made us very cynical as a society and that sense of the possibility of changing things has just frittered away. Maybe now that attitude is altering," says Labour's Chris Smith.

Lancaster University's Bronislaw Szerszynski is even more optimistic: "I think that people are different now, people demand more of authorities. Not just that people know more and view authorities as being intrinsically less trustworthy; nowadays people will ask much more. There has been a cultural change."

Some of those involved reckon DIY Culture has the potential to reach even further into the everyday life of Britain's communities. "More and more people are beginning to realise that there is something deeply amiss in the way that we live," says the journalist and author CJ Stone. "It is not just from necessity. Many people have food, shelter, TV, beer and cigarettes, but they are not happy. So it isn't necessity on that level. It comes from the deeper need to have a fuller life."

Adrian Harris, of the Dragon Environmental Network, agrees: "There is a growing awareness of spirituality. The penny appears to have finally dropped that consumerism doesn't satisfy your deepest needs. People are now saying, 'Hang on a second, we have got all these things that the adman says we should have and we are still not happy'."

Hew Beynon, Professor of Sociology at Manchester University, believes this opposition to consumerism is born out of necessity. "Growing numbers of people can no longer exert their rights by withdrawing their labour – either because they don't have jobs or because they are in occupations where there is no recognised trade union," he says. "Therefore they express their opposition to exploitation, unfairness and other aspects of modern society in the way they consume. This conscious decision about how they exist in a consumer society is one of the main avenues of real power left to them, whether it's through making rather than buying music, or establishing communes to grow food rather than going to the supermarket."

Whether this cultural change is sustainable remains to be seen. Some observers, particularly those who only see the direct action side of DIY, criticise the movement as being purely based on protest: only being against things and never offering viable answers. This may be true to some extent, but that's human nature: it is easier to build a strong movement of people united *against* something, than *for* something. The first priority is to stop the damage; the next is to decide what is needed instead.

Others criticise DIY for being just NIMBYism – the Not In My Back Yard syndrome, ultimately selfish and fundamentally conservative. This is also true to a certain extent and some activists don't think it is such a bad thing, providing the sentiment is widely shared. "If everybody is protesting against something being put in their back garden then it won't be in anybody's back garden," says former Green Party Euro and General Election candidate Shane Collins.

What is clear is that we are witnessing the biggest upsurge of direct action and alternative lifestyles for decades. This generation of activists are not simply asking for those in power to take note of their concerns, but are dealing directly with the issues – whether they be cruelty to animals or their own homelessness. And they can draw inspiration from abroad, such as the self-build communities for the homeless in Brazil, or attacks in India on the offices of multinational seed corporations that are attempting to patent some of the country's native plants and charge farmers for using them.

This book does not try to categorise or summarise this movement; it is too dynamic and diverse. We have just listened to what those involved have to say. DIY Culture is all around you: in your neighbourhood; in the countryside; in the protests you see on television; in the music in the street. Maybe one day you'll be part of it, if you're not already...

Illustration: Paul Render

Shoreham, Sussex, February 1995
Anti-live export campaigner

Photo: Andrew Testa

Animal Rights

"Activist, Anarchist, Extremist, Fanatic.
If that is what I am to be called,
because I care –
I shall wear each name with pride!"

The issue of animal welfare has hit a sensitive nerve with a wide and varied selection of the population, developing from a minority concern into a key political issue. People who had never participated in overtly political social protests suddenly found themselves risking life and limb in scuffles with police at the docksides, trying to stop huge lorries delivering their cargoes of live veal calves, lambs and sheep for export.

This is partly based on the traditional British sentimental attitude towards animals but there is something new as well: there has been a change in what people consider to be acceptable treatment of animals in modern agriculture and elsewhere. Years of sustained campaigning by animal rights organisations have created a public that is sensitised to the issues and unafraid of acting on their beliefs.

Middle class housewives and retired bank managers are being joined by young radicals in challenging the way big business treats animals. Traditional political activists envy the ability of the animal rights issue to unite such large numbers of people, but some also resent the use of this energy in what they see as a diversion from the main battle of tackling the capitalist system. Yet that is exactly what the protests against live exports of animals have done: they have challenged the right of big business to make profits out of the suffering of livestock and have hit the companies where it hurts – in the pocket.

Leaders of animal rights groups insist that those involved are very much aware of where their concerns fit into the wider picture. "What is happening now is that people have a more sophisticated approach because they have digested the green doctrine, the animal rights doctrine, feminism, racism, homophobia..." says Andrew Tyler, campaigns director of Animal Aid. "They can now recognise kindred spirits."

And, not all the campaigners are even vegetarians. "It is simply a case that we're against live exports; not meat eating, not dead exports," explains Jane, a demonstrator at Brightlingsea docks.

One of the successes of animal rights campaigning is that certain people are no longer content to finance an organisation to act on their behalf, they want to address the issues themselves. In the case of the live exports protests in 1995, the catalyst for action was circumstance. Animal rights groups succeeded, through some carefully-planned publicity campaigns and stunts, in exposing to public scrutiny the dark side of a trade that had being going since the 1950s.

The issue had been brought to public and Government attention numerous times before, but the situation had not improved much; temporary bans had been lifted and enforcement of European Union directives and welfare guidelines was poor.

This time around things turned out differently because more people suddenly cottoned on that live exports are cruel and unnecessary. They were appalled at standards during the long journeys (packed container lorries, inadequate food and water, poor conditions at lairages – the places the animals are kept before transportation) and at the fact that the animals were being sent to countries where their treatment in farms and slaughter houses can leave much to be desired.

"When you see for yourself the animals looking out of the lorries, there is no deceiving yourself with self-protective platitudes such as, 'It dosen't happen anymore', or 'It isn't as bad as people say'," says Liz Poole, a protester at Dover and other ports. "Those eyes aren't looking at some camera on a TV documentary, they're looking at you and pleading for help. That's the shocking reality that compels you to act."

Protesters questioned why animals have to be transported alive when most of them are to be sent to abattoirs on arrival. Most of the calves being exported to the continent are destined for tiny veal crates in which they have no room to move and where they will be kept in the dark and fed a restricted diet to create the prized white meat. This was seen as glaring hypocrisy given that veal crates have been banned in this country since 1990.

By November 1994 a strong public outcry had resulted in the major passenger ferry companies withdrawing their services from the animal exporters, forcing them to rely on private shipping companies. Since the trade was temporarily banned from Dover's docks, the exporters had to use ports such as Brightlingsea in Essex and Shoreham-By-Sea in Sussex, or fly out the animals from Coventry airport. Suddenly live exports became a visible issue for many more people.

Daily lorry loads of a sheep and calves passed through their main streets, right under residents' noses. What they saw shocked and appalled them. "We were walking along the promenade one night and saw some protesting going on so we went and had a look," explain Jill and Nick, two Shoreham residents. "We saw the lorries full of calves and sheep and read the literature… We've both been at it ever since, it is too hard to ignore." Or, as another protester puts it: "What these farmers don't understand is the emotional issue, it is a gut reaction, you can't help yourself when you see the calves."

In Dover, channel crossings can be made day and night, but in the smaller ports crossings were only possible at high tide. Therefore everyone knew when the containers of animals were coming through and could be ready. The streets were small, making it relatively easy to block the convoys. Thus, when no-one in authority seemed to take any notice of local objections to the trade, direct action became a very effective alternative.

Outrage against animal exports led to some incredible scenes: thousands of people joining together to change what sickened them. This new wave of animal welfare campaigning included people who could not be dismissed with the usual labels of "rent-a-mob, dole-scrounger, hippy, anarchist". It contained an agreeably mixed bag of participants and plenty of them were ABC1 Tory voters of impeccable law-abiding credentials who would probably normally be the mainstay of the local Neighbourhood Watch scheme. The cliché of "I've never done this type of thing before" could have been invented for animal protests.

The protester against live exports
Liz Poole, now in her thirties, has lived in England nearly all her life; she is a self-employed craftsworker, living near Canterbury, making furniture and picture frames. When she first went down to the lairages – the places where animals are kept before being transported – she was physically sick for eight hours because of the overcrowding and suffering of the animals; from then on she became a dedicated campaigner. Before last year, she had always been aware of issues but had never joined a group, now she is a member of half a dozen.

She goes on actions and protests between one and three times a week. She believes it is important to attack the issue from all angles: she has written more than 250 letters to the local and national press, all the European embassies, pop stars, supermarkets, ferry companies, local and other MPs, and the Ministry of Agriculture Fisheries and Food.

"Farming has always bothered me, ever since I saw a poster when I was young. I used to get answers to my letters but nothing happened, they always shift the responsibility to someone else."

"This is Brightlingsea Against Live Exports," intoned the well-spoken voice of housewife Maria Wilby on her answerphone during the 1995 actions. "We hope this is a peaceful week. Be there from 8.30am." Protesters were urged to dress warmly and hot drinks and refreshments would usually be laid on. However, the well-mannered organisation didn't undermine the determination to stop the lorries. Where possible people tried to block the route; when the police got there first, they shouted from the sidelines, a mass of home-made banners filling the streets of the small seaside town. No Socialist Workers Party placards or "Kick out the Tories" slogans here; the messages were heart-felt and non-clichéd, speaking of cruelty and greed.

"I go protesting with trepidation," says Liz Poole. "I feel sick with a mixture of adrenaline and horror. Yet I feel comfortable in the crowd of protesters; I know they're real people, people I've needed to meet all my life. The instant rapport with strangers is overwhelming."

Joan Le Mesurier in the book, The Siege of Shoreham, summed up the atmosphere: "This is the thing that the British, once spurred into action, are best at; it's the Dunkirk spirit down there in Shoreham, alive and kicking and we mustn't let it die because if we can't do something to change this vile trade, then we are doomed to greed and indifference."

But still, you didn't expect to see middle-aged couples and the older generation in sensible coats hurling abuse outside a farmer's door, or lying down on the road in front of lorries, smashing windscreens and letting down tyres. Many of them looked more as if they were on their way to a Parish Council meeting than to a demonstration. They were hardly fly-by-night trouble-makers looking for a cause; the people involved in live export protests were much more likely to live close by and were out there every day.

Their passion even took some of the organisers by surprise. "If people feel that's the way to stop them, by smashing windscreens, that is up to them. If we can stop them by the regulations, that is just as well, actually better," says Trevor Love of Compassion in World Farming. "I would rather it were stopped on regulations than by people risking their lives and endangering others. I would rather it were done through the courts and the law of this country." But it wasn't.

Coventry, February 1995
Protest to stop exports of sheep and calves to Europe
Photo: Andrew Testa

Shoreham Harbour, 1995
Photo: Adrian Short

Brightlingsea, Essex, January 1995
Protesters try to stop lorries full
of sheep from reaching the port
at Brightlingsea

Photo: Andrew Testa

Brightlingsea, Essex, January 1995
Brightlingsea residents try to stop
the police forcing a shipment of sheep
through the town

Photo: Andrew Testa

The animal welfare campaigner
Margaret Gibbins is 58 and lives in Cornwall with her husband who is a retired branch manager of Lloyds bank. They have three grown-up children and have always lived in the West Country as her husband's interest was in rural and agricultural banking. Before becoming actively involved in animal rights campaigning, she had planned a retirement consisting of bird, dolphin and whale watching with the Cornwall Wildlife Trust. Now her days are taken up with monitoring her local livestock market, attending demonstrations and writing to those in authority to demand change.

"I was in the flower arranging class and ladies choir, though they probably wouldn't have me back now."

A reply to one of Margaret Gibbins's letters

Dear Mrs Gibbins,

Thank you for your letter to the Prime Minister of the 25th February 1996. I have been asked to reply on his behalf.

The Prime Minister does not share your view that this Government is rotten to the core. Neither the examples you cite: live exports or the Scott report in any sense justifies your accusation.

Yours Sincerely

Rodick Brown
*On behalf
of the Prime Minister
John Major*

The scale of the protests in 1995 also took the establishment by surprise. "They seem to have no leader, no organising committee, not even a press officer. And yet they are capable of mounting demonstrations in five widely-separated parts of the kingdom simultaneously," complained an editorial in The Financial Times. "Plymouth, Shoreham, Brightlingsea, Coventry and Swansea have all sometimes on the same day needed extravagant and highly unpopular diversions of police resources."

In Brightlingsea, it's estimated that 3,000 out of a population of 8,000 came out to demonstrate against live exports. During the protests, more than 170 convoys went through the town at a cost of £2.25 million in extra policing. At the peak of the activity, 300 officers were required to keep the peace and there were frequent battles between the police and protesters, resulting in hundreds of arrests. Ten months of protest in Brightlingsea ended in October 1995, when exports were suspended.

At Shoreham, according to the alternative newsletter Schnews, Inner London and Surrey forces were used in a huge operation, lining the harbour with a mile and a half of riot vans and buses containing 1,500 police. The nightly presence, which outnumbered protesters six to one at times, shocked and angered local people.

Many who were involved in the anti-live export campaigns found themselves on the wrong side of the law for the first time in their lives and experienced what it was like to be treated as a threat to society. The following, from Bernard Denyer, a participant in the protests at Shoreham, illustrates the shock that awaited people when they got to the picket lines: "Stony faced officers with camera trained on the crowd. Tears flow from men, women and youngsters alike, tears of grief, rage and frustration… This is Britain in 1995. I wonder what happened to all my cherished beliefs and youthful ideals. Is this really a glimpse of the future?"

Or from another Shoreham protester: "Like many other people I had never protested about anything before although I knew I should have done. This time it was different. I have seen things during this protest I thought I would never be witness to: people arrested for throwing orange peel, a sweet wrapper, for lobbing an egg at a driver who was laughing at us as he passed. Knowing what is possible down there, it came as no surprise that I saw a woman in her sixties pushed over by a policeman before the convoy came through."

That kind of treatment wasn't uncommon at Shoreham. "I asked the policeman for his identity number and he grabbed me by the hair and threw me across the road," remembers Ann Baker-Smith, a 57-year-old library assistant.

Live exports and the authorities' response to the protests forced some participants to question wider aspects of the functioning of Britain. Andrew Tyler of Animal Aid reckons this awakening is very common. "We talk to lots of people and the message you get, over and over is: 'My life has changed, I used to trust the police and now they think that I am a nutcase. Now I just feel guilty that I didn't realise before, I wish I had realised it 20 or 30 years ago.' It takes real courage to admit that at an age when you are supposed to be settling down. We are all conditioned, particularly when we grow up in conservative areas."

Animal welfare has helped forge connections between people who would never have come into contact before. Many of the older demonstrators were impressed by the energy of the younger activists – and vice versa. The protests built cross-generational understanding of issues such as restrictions on the right to protest, to hold raves and to enter private land which were brought in by the Criminal Justice and Public Order Act 1994.

The live exports campaign was particularly visual and focused in one place, so it was relatively easy to keep it in the mainstream media – an important element in maintaining pressure to force changes in policy. Animal rights groups have become increasingly adept at using the mainstream and alternative media as a campaigning tool.

"We have learned over the last 20 years that there is no point in existing in a ghetto, it's no good talking to ourselves," says Animal Aid's Andrew Tyler. "You have to talk to the public and to do this you have to use the mass channels of communication which are the mainstream media. You have to use the tools that allow you to assert yourself: it can be a £400 PC, a camcorder or a tape recorder.

"You care, you bear witness, you come back with an account and then you disseminate it. You have to be clear about the facts, you can't exaggerate, you can't libel and you must support it with official statistics, because otherwise the meat industry will call you a liar and a fantasist and attack your character. But these slurs are becoming more and more difficult to sustain, because ordinary people, not just the traditional radical stock, are joining the action."

The animal rights groups are keen to sustain the energy generated around the exports of live animals and use it to bring about wider improvements in the treatment of animals by Britain's farming industry. Market Watch is a nation-wide scheme which encourages people concerned with animal welfare to take evidence for themselves by walking around livestock markets, taking notes and sometimes filming or photographing. Participants know the legislation off by heart, they know what is illegal and what isn't. They don't demonstrate, they just go to observe and gather evidence. Something anyone can do.

"We have found out that only four markets are actually licensed for live exports, yet many more are involved in the trade," says Margaret Gibbins, a Market Watch activist in the West country. "So in fact the police are aiding and abetting an illegal act. The trading standards agree. There is so much breaking of the law."

Those who are at the receiving end of the protests – farmers, export companies, supermarkets – often attribute them to "ignorant urbanites" who don't understand the ways of the countryside, the basics of farming, or where food comes from. "We're right down there at the very sharp end of the wedge with people coming round causing criminal damage, day and night and being a bloody nuisance," says one farmer. "And on top of that most of them can't even produce a rational argument for what they're doing. It's complete nonsense."

Many of the media commentators sympathise. "From the other end of the telescope, the minority still working on the land stare back at the cities and suburbs and see a haze of hypocrisy and ignorance," wrote Andrew Marr in The Independent. "They see consumers wanting cheap, interesting and varied food, without being ready to spend much time or money on it. Yet the majority who prefer life that way descend into moral spasm whenever they glimpse the consequences of their impossible demands."

However the live exports protests did awaken many people to these contradictions. The scares over Bovine Spongiform Encephalopathy (BSE or "mad cow disease") showed that not only can our industrialised food production system be cruel, it can be dangerous, too. A return to locally-produced food with animals reared in free-range conditions would be popular, environmentally friendly and could boost rural economies – if people were prepared to pay for it.

But many farmers doubt whether this is practical. "You're trying to convert the wrong people," complains one. "Unfortunately this country is in the hands of five major supermarket chains who pay lip service to animal welfare. The farmers only produce what the supermarkets and housewives buy.

"We're not advocating factory farming, in fact all it has done is to tie farmers to the bank, we all know that. If you quietly ask, most farmers long for the days of what we used to call dog and stick, without the financial pressures. But it is a very big business and it's been driven that way because of the collateral of land prices and the ever upward spiral of growth – borrow more, earn more – all of which are a factor of modern society. Your organisations are making personal attacks on farmers and you're not actually looking at what is happening in the whole world."

And that means that the animal rights groups need to spread their influence still further to build widespread consumer boycotts. It's a form of direct action that everyone can engage in and it's often one of the most effective.

At the other end of the spectrum are the exploits of the more radical animal rights groups such as hunt saboteurs or the Animal Liberation Front storm troopers who set fire to abattoirs and attack laboratories that use animals for testing. These people are still seen by some as the lunatic fringe and their concerns go unheeded by those in power.

Over the past decade the issue of blood sports has been taken into Parliament and turned down so many times that it has incensed people into turning away from letter writing to take up direct action. "A huge percentage of the population disagrees with bloodsports but the Government just doesn't listen," says Reuben, a hunt saboteur from Cambridge. "The people who hunt are in a position of social and political power and that is the reason why it hasn't stopped."

The hunt saboteur
Reuben, who is 30, was born in south London and spent most of his childhood in care. He then travelled for a while before studying psychology at Cambridge Technology College when he was in his twenties. This was when he was most involved in hunt sabbing – stopping the local fox hunt. He was homeless for the four years of his college course and, as well as being involved in sabbing, worked as an outreach counsellor dealing with the homeless, the mentally ill and drug abusers.

"Greenpeace was behind the sabotaging of international hunting of whales and seals, however nothing was actually being done about fox hunting in this country. Some people wanted to do things themselves, in a hands-on practical way, so hunt sabbing began."

SUFFERING

Trawsfynydd, Wales, March 1995
A fox killed by hounds is left in the
fork of a tree to rot

Photo: Andrew Testa

Surrey Union Hunt, Surrey 1993
Saboteur runs among the fox hounds
to throw them off the scent

Photo: Andrew Testa

HUNT SABBING CONSISTS OF MUCH MORE THAN
STANDING ON PICKET LINES, IT REQUIRES REAL
PHYSICAL ENERGY AND STRATEGY

Crawley and Horsham Hunt, Sussex 1995
Insults fly between a hunter and saboteurs
after some hunt followers and riders staged
an eloborate ambush which resulted in three
saboteurs being hospitalised and photographers
from The Guardian and the New Musical
Express being attacked by hunt followers

Photo: Andrew Testa

This has prompted activists to say: "If I don't take action, nobody will." "I used to be interested in arguing all the politics, now I think: 'Just do it'," Says Darna, a hunt sab from Birmingham. "We are not there to philosophise or argue, or to change society on a higher level, we are just there on the day to literally save a fox's life."

Hunt sabs are usually well organised and selfdisciplined, not just hippies and the unemployed. "Look at us – there are two teachers and a post-graduate student," says Dave, a colleague of Darna's. "We're not just dole-dodgers and students who will grow out of it. But we're also not an organisation; we're just a means of communicating around the country."

Shoreham, Sussex, January 1995
Live export protest

Photo: Adrian Short

Old Surrey and Berstow Hunt, Surrey 1994
A saboteur makes his views known

Photo: Andrew Testa

"It tends to be the older generation and the professionals who write the letters and campaign, whilst the active sabbing is left to those with the physical ability to do it," says Reuben. "Hunt sabbing consists of much more than standing on picket lines, it requires real physical energy and strategy. Different people are assigned to different tactics: horn blowers, chargers who run into the hunt and confuse the dogs, people on gizmos (stereos with recordings of hounds), and drivers who trace the hunt."

They must be worrying people in power because hunt saboteurs were one of the targets of sections in the Criminal Justice and Public Order Act 1994 that make trespass a criminal offence. Many of the first arrests under the Act were against saboteurs, yet it is usually the saboteurs that come off worse in any confrontation with the men and women of the fox hunt. There have been numerous cases of hunt sabs being beaten by the hunters and their minders. A couple of sabs have even been killed while trying to stop a hunt.

On a more positive note, in April 1997 the National Trust banned stag hunting on its land because of public opinion and several Labour MPs have promised to introduce laws to stop bloodsports.

Hunt sabbing is the soft end of the more radical animal rights actions, according to Annette Tibbles, who was sentenced to four years in London's Holloway Prison for planning a wave of arson attacks on meat firms in the south Midlands. She reckons the more hard-line movements much bigger than reported in the press. The Animal Liberation Front encourages supporters to wage a financial war by actions such as smashing the windows of Boots chemists – because of their alleged involvement in testing drugs and cosmetics on animals – and attacking butchers' shops.

Tibbles rejects the "eco-terrorist" label given to many of the more radical activists, who are accused of violent acts such as placing car bombs under the cars of scientists engaged in animal experiments. "Animal liberationists want to stop the suffering of all creatures," she protests, "so we're unlikely to want to hurt humans."

Sometimes the action involves one person doing risky undercover investigations – like Chris Iles who spent nearly two years in animal laboratories in London. He did it because he didn't believe the claims that animals used in experiments and testing were being protected by the law. When he asked the Home Office about checks on practices they were unresponsive and unco-operative. Since there was no other way of getting hold of evidence, he investigated himself. His report, which documented the animals' suffering, shocked people, made national headlines and interested several MPs.

"We suspected that the claims that animals were being protected under the law just weren't true and we were not content with the sweeping statements by the Home Office inspectors," he explains. "There really wasn't any other way of getting hold of evidence apart from going undercover."

An Undercover Britain secretly-filmed documentary on Channel 4 in March 1997 reinforced Chris's report by showing how inspectors appeared to turn a blind eye to ill treatment of beagle hounds used for drug testing. Again the findings caused a public outcry, but there was no official action.

Despite the wide range of issues and approaches to animal rights, there is a common thread: they force many participants to take up other issues. "I've been kept in a box for 58 years and had never dared to question things – I was busy bringing up my children," admits Margaret Gibbins. "But when you step out of your box you suddenly realise that you don't live in a democracy, it is just a word."

Roads and Transport

"When a government tries to destroy your home, your community, your environment and your livelihood without even so much as an apology, you don't just stand by and watch. I shall defend my home to the very last."

Mick Thompson, resident of Claremont Road which was demolished to make way for an extension of the M11 motorway in east London

Since the beginning of this century, the systematic gashing of our countryside to make way for new roads had almost become accepted: a necessary price to pay for the "personal freedom" promised by car ownership. But then road building got out of hand in the 1980s as a result of the Conservative government's aversion to public transport – particularly state-owned public transport. By 1991 the Cabinet had quietly nodded through a billowing construction programme on the basis of dodgy predictions that car travel would increase by 130 per cent over the next 25 years. Contracts worth £23 billion would be ample reward for the British Road Federation and the Road Hauliers Association who counted among their members many of the major business supporters of the Conservative Party.

It was the biggest road-building programme ever attempted in Britain, threatening, among other things, 161 Sites of Special Scientific Interest and more than 800 important archaeological areas. This huge increase in scale meant many communities would be affected.

The problems associated with the building of roads are well known, but until the construction proposals of the early 1990s they had been easier to ignore than to acknowledge. Car use has become a habit that is extremely difficult to break or even to question. There is also big money at stake: the motor industry and road construction companies are pillars of the British economy and major employers. Thus, a new road has become an indisputable fact of life, something you accept; until, of course, it's in your neighbourhood.

"There were so many areas of outstanding natural beauty, people's houses and communities threatened… everywhere from the white cliffs of Dover to the tenements of Glasgow," says Emma Must, co-ordinator of the anti-roads group Alarm UK. "The Tory Government had tried to do too much. It had

gone too far in encroaching on people's lives and the places people valued, be it their own homes or their green spaces. There was bound to be an uprising."

Hundreds of local groups sprung up in opposition to the programme of new roads, bypasses and "improvements". They represented the growing number of people who were no longer willing to put up with an unsustainable transport policy that continues to pave over the countryside without offering viable alternatives. To them, road building epitomised many environmental and social issues: over-population, poor quality of life, urban sprawl, increasing pollution, decaying inner cities and conflicting land use.

Until recently, most people opposing road schemes had done so within the accepted structures devised by the Department of Transport or the Scottish or Welsh Offices. The Department (or Scottish or Welsh equivalent) would put its route options out for public consultation and people would be urged to tick a box to indicate which one they favoured. Then came the Public Inquiry, where protesters were urged to make polite, well-reasoned arguments outlining why they objected. Most did and almost all were unsuccessful: the vast majority of Public Inquiries have come down in favour of building the road, although they occasionally demand alterations to take some objections into account.

This process was turned on its head during the rush of proposed schemes in the early 1990s when there was a realisation that the Department of Transport's framework for protest was not designed to address real alternatives to a new road but was, in most cases, merely paying lip service to democracy. Campaigners therefore began to set out their own – DIY style – methods of objection which challenged the traditional rules of the game and put the Department and its officials on the defensive.

**Top: Twyford Down
December 1992**

**Bottom: M11 Link Road
September 1994**
Protestors crying during the felling
of Busk Wood in east London

Photos: Alex MacNaughton

The full-time activist
Shane Collins, is 35 and has lived
in London for 14 years. He has been
in the Green Party since 1989 and
stood as a candidate in a couple
of general elections and a European
Parliament election.

Shane was a major force in setting
up the Cooltan community and
campaigning centre in Brixton in
1991. It was from the Cooltan Centre
that the anti-car group Reclaim the
Streets and the Freedom Network
began. He got involved in Earth
First! in 1992 around the time of the
protests at Twyford Down against
the extension of the M3 motorway
and is part of Ecotrip which operates
within the green movement to
try and make green politics more
relevant to young people.

He used to work in film production
as a clapper loader, then later
directing, but gradually moved
into full-time political activism.

*"I got involved in green issues after
reading Seeing Green by Jonathan
Porritt while in Brazil,"* he says.
*"I had expected to feel sorry
for people but ended up learning
a lot, particularly that poverty
is far more bearable if it's shared,
rather than individualised as it
is in Britain. It's important that we
reclaim responsibility for our own
lives and part of that is protecting
the environment and communities
from unnecessary road schemes."*

Most of the campaigns were rooted in local communities, linked by umbrella groups such as Alarm UK and Road Alert!, using background research and support from well-established environmental organisations including Transport 2000, Friends of the Earth and Greenpeace. The Department of Transport found itself confronted by a movement which had no visible head but many local leaders.

Each campaign gathered reams of terrifying statistics about the extent and implications of Britain's love affair with the car:

- **Every mile of motorway takes up 25 acres of land and uses 250,000 tonnes of sand and gravel;**
- **Cars are responsible for 51 per cent of UK emissions of nitrogen oxides which irritate the lungs and create acid rain;**
- **Cars are responsible for a fifth of the UK's production of greenhouse gases such as carbon dioxide which are responsible for global warming;**
- **One in seven children in London has asthma, and traffic pollution has been shown to be one of the causes;**
- **An estimated 15 million people in Britain are suffering illnesses related to traffic pollution.**

Armed with these and much more, local groups lobbied their MPs, wrote letters, went to the planning inquiries for each road scheme and held demonstrations, convinced that the weight of their arguments would win the day. Many plans for new roads were scuppered at an early stage through the sheer weight of opposing evidence: the Hereford eastern bypass; the second Tamar crossing near Plymouth; the Preston southern and western bypass; the east London river crossing through Oxleas Wood; the M1-M62 link in Yorkshire; the M62 relief road in Manchester; the Worthing bypass. People had taken on the might of the Department of Transport and won.

But in other cases, the channels of democracy seemed to have silted up.

"I had tried writing to my MP and the Scottish Office for facts, but they were so arrogant, they just didn't want to consult with us," says Jean, a resident of Pollok in south west Glasgow where the £51 million four-lane M8-Ayr link road will decimate Pollok Park and sever housing estates from the green belt. "They just wanted to rule over us and totally ignore our requests."

This was when objections entered a new, more visible phase: non-violent direct action in which protesters tried physically to stop the road construction process. "When a bulldozer rips up the countryside, you don't just sit at home and write to your MP. Nor do you simply hold a banner or go on a march demanding change from a fundamentally flawed political process," explains Sam a member of the radical anti-roads group Reclaim the Streets. "You go out and do something about it."

Before the summer of 1993 most of us had never heard of Twyford Down, Oxleas Wood or Claremont Road. But these were the first astonishing episodes in the long-running saga of communities versus concrete in which people who were frustrated that their arguments had been ignored opted for more unconventional tactics. Since then our vocabulary has expanded to include Pollok Estate, Middle Oak near Newbury, Fairmile in Devon and many others.

"I came from a background of concerned but respectable and restrained involvement. I spent years in formal committees of preservation groups, not achieving very much," says Chris Gillham of the Twyford Down Association which attempted to stop the extension of the M3 motorway through historically and ecologically important chalk land in Hampshire. "Twyford Down is the justification, whenever it is needed, for non-violent direct action. The system allowed us to spend decades in argument, and huge sums of money, making an intellectually unshakeable case, only for the system to brush it all aside. When you hear the brazen words 'democratic process' and 'rule of law', reply quietly 'Twyford Down'."

In the case of the M11 link road in east London, a powerful demonstration of community action was triggered when developers boarded off the common land of George Green in Wanstead to prepare for the road. This southern extension of the M11 was estimated to save eight minutes driving time at a cost of demolishing more than 300 houses. Protesters warned that they were ready to fight every step of the way.

TUNNELLING FOR BEGINNERS (Don't try this at home! Ed)

Muppet Dave, May 1997

"To build a tunnel you take a shovel and start digging – down. Dig a shaft and from the bottom dig your main tunnel. Shore it up by putting two pieces of hard wood or treated wood (pallets aren't strong enough) against either side and across the top. The amount of shoring depends on the ground: in clay, which we have at the No Runway 2 site, you can go quite far without shoring. We'll probably take it out as we're being evicted to make it more difficult for the bailiffs to get us.

You usually stop digging downwards when you hit the water table – unless you want to dig through it to make a sump, then dig upwards again. This creates a chamber filled with water. During evictions you put on a wet suit and swim through the chamber to the other side. The bailiffs then have to pump out the water and shore up the chamber to get to you. It's been thought of but we haven't done it yet.

Once you have a central shaft, other people move in and start digging in different directions. In my tunnel, called the Cake Hole, there are people digging in five different directions. It takes three times as long to get the dirt out of the tunnel as it does to dig it. We're now 50 feet down and the tunnels just run and run. They're like corkscrews, they go up and down, round corners – all to make it more difficult to evict us.

You then put doors along the tunnel: concrete doors, metal doors, doors of reinforced wood with metal and concrete mix – anything. At Fairmile it took the bailiffs a day to get through each door.

I've now been living in a tunnel at Manchester for about four weeks and I stay underground most of the time.

It's about 17 degrees centigrade down there, quite comfortable really. We pump air down the tunnel using a car battery and keep food ready for the eviction – we might be here about a year or they might come in two weeks. You're actually safer during an eviction than living there day to day because you've got all the emergency services round you."

Muppet Dave, 30, is a former traveller, soldier; veteren of Newbury and Fairmile, who is now involved in the No Runway 2 protest camp at Manchester Airport.

| 1 | 2 | 4 |
| | 3 | 5 |

1 Newbury By Pass, December 1995
  Protester in tunnel
2 Claremont Road, November 1994
  Protester on roof
3 Twyford Down, May 1993
4 M11, Wanstead, January 1994
5 Newbury By Pass, January 1996
  Protesters in the trees at Pen Wood

Photos: Alex MacNaughton

The international award-winner
Emma Must, former librarian and now worker for the anti-roads group Alarm UK, is 30 and lives in London. She got involved in roads protests in 1992 when she passed Twyford Down on the train every day on the way to and from work and could see the hill being stripped. She grew up there and had a very strong attachment to the area. She then met some of the Dongas Tribe who had settled there as a protest and some of the local people who were still campaigning, and it all started from there.

Before Twyford Down Emma had been thinking of training to be an English teacher but involvement in the roads campaign changed her life, making her much more political and more concerned with the wider world. However, she feels it is important to combine the often intense campaigning with other aspects of your life.

"You do have to look after yourself, otherwise you can't do anything. You do have to go out occasionally get pissed and let off steam, pace yourself and do things that you enjoy as well, otherwise you lose the balanced perspective which is vital."

In 1995 she won the Goldman Environmental Award for Europe for grass roots environmental campaigning, but said it was really for the whole anti-roads movement. Most of the £45,000 prize money went to provide facilities for Alarm UK and its direct action arm Road Alert!

"A small number of people can make a difference if they work together. You have much more effect if you find other people who have the same goals. But you have to be realistic, it is impossible to change the whole underlying structure. Just take one thing at a time. I don't really know if I have a sufficiently wide perspective to judge if things are going to get better – that bothers me, but at least it is honest."

"Some were there to voice their opposition to a corrupt government perceived to be answering to their 'friends' in the road lobby, instead of answering the people. Others were there to protest against a car culture which pollutes the air and destroys the countryside, people's homes and people's lives. Others still, were there to demonstrate about global or civil liberty issues; this road scheme symbolised it all." (Taken from the first issue of Frontline, about Claremont Road).

On 6 November 1993 local residents and campaigners spontaneously tore down the fences around George Green in front of stunned police and security guards. The land and an ancient sweet chestnut tree which stood there were occupied for over a month in an attempt to delay the construction work.

Over the following weeks, 1,200 people took part in daily site invasions, stopping the bulldozers through peaceful protest action. Embarrassed policemen had to haul pensioners away from work areas and school children spurred on weary campaigners; active members of the local community, such as the school lollipop lady, joined in.

The battles at the M11 and against several other major road schemes demonstrated just how far protesters are prepared to go.

"There is a man digging a tunnel which will cave in killing him and anyone else foolhardy enough to use it if heavy machinery moves onto the common," says Clare, one of the protesters against the Newbury bypass on the A34. "People are ready to die for this land."

Or, as Stuart, one of the climbers that helped create a network of tree houses and aerial walkways in the wood that was threatened by the bypass put it: "You come down here and get involved. I found myself climbing in the trees and setting up rope walkways, yet when I first came down I thought I'd just show a few people some knots and how to do things safely. But you can't just stand by, not if you have any compassion. You have to get involved. It's a gut emotion."

The tenacity and inventiveness of direct action meant the Department of Transport and the construction firms had to resort to long and expensive eviction processes to get the protesters off the sites. A variety of media-friendly stunts, meanwhile, gave journalists an ample supply of stories that kept the campaigns in the news: fortressed streets, barricaded houses filled with rubble, tree villages, aerial walkways, webs of nets and underground tunnels.

Twyford Down, February 1993
Emma Must leading protest march

Photo: Alex MacNaughton

"Direct action is closely linked to the media. You can have an action but the country won't know unless the media are there to make the headlines," says Alisdair Palmer a journalist at The Spectator. "People are no longer lobbying by letter, they are lobbying by protesting and capturing media attention."

However, although the press and broadcasting coverage of the major actions was welcome, it tended to overshadow the weeks or months of careful planning that went into them, says Emma Must of Alarm UK. "The media-friendly direct action has dramatised and highlighted what is going on, but it is only the tip of the iceberg. Underneath there are 250 groups beetling away at a much earlier stage, before the bulldozers have moved in," she explains. "They're holding events and developing alternatives to roads, but these don't get picked up by the press. Direct action is what the media want. I find it very frustrating that the only way that you can actually get any protest covered is by direct action."

Initially the mainstream environmental groups such as Friends of the Earth and Greenpeace, didn't openly support the direct action, largely because they feared they might lose members or face costly legal battles for encouraging people to break the law. Later, at the Newbury Bypass, Friends of the Earth took an active role, organising large demonstrations and encouraging their members to support the campaigns. However, there is still an uneasy relationship between the DIY activists, who will often risk everything, and the larger organisations taking a safer approach.

"In Newbury, FoE gave a lot of funding and sent legal observers, but its structure prevented full involvement," explains Ian, an activist with Reclaim the Streets. "FoE would stop anything dead that might cause legal difficulties. For instance, there was a problem with bail conditions and a lot of us were prevented from protesting. I was going to get round it by setting up a mythical job with a friend in Newbury, but FoE advised businesses against it."

Like the animal rights movement, the roads protests have been able to unite a wide range of people from contrasting backgrounds and with very different politics and ideologies. As that bastion of the establishment, The Economist, put it: "Protesting about new roads has become that rarest of British phenomena, a truly populist movement drawing supporters from all walks of life."

Some of the opposition came from quarters not associated with radical action – such as the Townswomen's Guild. Its chairwoman, Joan Helm, joined a major march and lobby of Parliament in January 1997 because: "We want fresh air and freedom instead of fumes and frustration."

One of the first times this kaleidoscope of people came together was in the summer of 1993 during the attempt to stop the extension of the M3 motorway through Twyford Down in Hampshire. "There were the Dongas who looked very alternative and were basically living outside, pursuing a very low impact lifestyle," says Emma Must. "They had a very, very different way of living to the people in Winchester; yet there was no question of any awkwardness. When the Friends of Twyford Down met the Dongas tribe they realised that these people were talking about direct action and that it was a good idea. They were really grateful that people were prepared to commit themselves that much to try and stop the road."

However, this utopian ideal of young and old, conservative and anarchist, conformist and non-conformist building mutual understanding and appreciation in the interests of a greater cause didn't always happen. Sometimes there has been direct hostility to the DIYers from the existing residents who regard them as outsiders trying to interfere in established communities without any understanding of local problems.

"I don't appreciate anyone coming here to protest to save rural England if they are not willing to live here," says a farmer living near the proposed Preston bypass which was shelved. "It is the people who live here who have to travel on these roads and some of them are just plain dangerous."

The same suspicions can exist in urban areas. At the M8-Ayr link road in Pollok, south Glasgow, it took a while for residents to connect with the protesters. The amount of local input was not as big as it would have been simply because of this image of environmentalist extremists and dreadlocked hippies, explains Ronnie, a worker at the Solidarity Centre community project. "It is a sad fact of life that those folks do tend to chase 'normal' people away... yet the road is going to affect everyone in Glasgow."

M11, East London, November 1994
Local resident joins the protests

Photo: Alex MacNaughton

The housewife
Amanda Martin is a former lawyer who has not practised professionally since the birth of her children (Thomas,12 and Ruth, 5). Now in her thirties, she has been active since 1993 in the campaign started by her village against the proposed £300 million M4 Newport relief road – a 13 mile, six-lane highway which will destroy four sites of special scientific interest in the Gwent levels, one of the few remaining unspoilt wetlands in Britain.

Amanda has just completed a masters degree in Urban and Regional Transport to give herself a wider perspective on transport issues. The village has commissioned its own study to address long-term alternatives to the road, looking at how local journeys, such as commuting, school runs and shopping trips, could be switched to public transport. The campaign has had some support from local businesses.

"This has never been a NIMBY campaign. We believe that it is not enough to wave placards and shout about stopping a road, you've got to look further than that. I've begun to realise how car culture affects society and people's behaviour towards each other. How can a community function properly when they only see each other through a windscreen?"

Camden, North London, May 1995
Reclaim the Streets turn a
traffic-clogged road into a no-car
zone for a street party

Photo: Nick Cobbing

Greenwich, South London
Protesters on top of a tripod used
to block the road

Photo: Nick Cobbing

London, Summer 1995
Cyclists go back to the spot where
a young cyclist was killed by a skip
lorry. They occupied the junction
in remembrance and in protest at
traffic congestion and pollution

Photo: Nick Cobbing

However, according to Ronnie's colleague Lindsay, the cultural differences were overcome as people got to know each other. "The kind of alienation that existed dissipated," she explains. "Now many of the housing schemes have their own autonomous campaigning organisations and there has been a lot of support from the local people for the road protesters." This included about 50 children from the local estates who came down to the protest site regularly.

"They were saying: "This shouldn't be built, this is our land, it belongs to us, our heritage'," says Lyndsay, a young Pollok resident. "At one point the headmaster of one of the secondaries locked the gate of the school because the children were spending so much time protesting: the children reacted by going on strike for two weeks."

The protests are widely acknowledged to have been at least partially responsible for the Government's decision in 1995 to cancel a third of the proposed road building programme: 77 schemes were scrapped and 100 put on hold. However, there are still numerous major schemes under construction or planned, so the campaigns continue, often broadening out to tackle wider aspects of transport, such as the second runway being built at Manchester airport. In early 1996, 550 people closed Whatley Quarry in Somerset for a day to protest against proposals to extend it. At 250 acres it is already the biggest quarry in Europe and provides stone for most of the new road building in Britain. Protesters caused an estimated £55,000 of damage – which did not go down well with residents or workers.

"I wish you would all get responsible jobs so you would stop coming here and stopping us from doing ours," said Whatley Quarry's foreman at the time. But Shane Collins of Earth First, one of the organisers of the occupation, had a ready reply: "One day when we all have responsible jobs that don't damage the Earth, we won't have to come here and protest."

At the lighter end of the scale, Reclaim the Streets and Critical Mass hold fairly regular "dis-organisation" stunts including huge colourful street parties in different traffic-choked parts of London such as Camden and Islington. The aim is to win back the streets for pedestrians and cyclists: jugglers, mime artists and fire eaters entertain the crowd and picnic tables provide food. Meanwhile rush-hour motorists fume.

Reclaim the Streets don't just put out a negative anti-car message. They want to show people the links between car culture and environmental and social problems. "Cars are not a solution that would ever have been chosen collectively by a society," says Phil, a member of the group. "By their very nature they represent a purely individual solution, but they're not intrinsically wrong… We're using the metaphor of a car to illustrate a variety of things: pollution, congestion, urban planning, public space."

One of the group's more serious events – traffic diversions in the highly polluted Greenwich High Street during rush hour – attracted considerable local support. "My kids have to go into the playground every day for an hour and breathe this muck, they're getting asthma. I think what Reclaim the Streets is doing is marvellous," says Shirley Broad, headteacher of a Greenwich school and a member of GASP, the local anti-pollution campaign.

Reclaim the Streets' occupation of the M40 in west London involved digging up the road surface to plant trees, causing an estimated £30,000 of damage.

Reclaim the Streets has now spread to many other towns and cities including Reading, Cardiff, Blackburn, Oxford, Southampton, Brighton and Nottingham. Some of its support overlaps with the UK branch of Critical Mass, the cyclists' direct action movement which started in San Francisco as an informal bike ride by 50 people. In cities across Britain, militant cyclists regularly come together to demonstrate, celebrate and reclaim the streets. A tumultuous procession of cyclists, from the hard-core anarchist to the city business man, ruling over the motor car, creating havoc by having their own way for an hour or two.

"As far as I am concerned it is about saying that London is a wonderful place at 6 o'clock on a Friday afternoon," says Patrick Field a spokesperson for Critical Mass. "It's about saying: I'm not rushing off to somewhere different because this is so horrible – this is where I live."

However, it still seems that roads protests only deeply influence those directly affected by a particular road. As an editorial in The Observer put it: "Before we all rush to the barricades let us all not be starry eyed about human nature. There is no evidence yet of any real transformation in attitudes. People want to end pollution, but to keep their cars, to have better public services, but to pay no taxes."

In other words they're just NIMBYs: the Not in My Back Yard people who want to stop a particular route being forged through a treasured local area but would not bother if it was somewhere else. To a certain extent this is true, but Britain is a collection of backyards and as the campaigns evolved, their arguments and strategies began to address wider issues.

Many of the protests may have begun as a simple stance against a road being built through a particular area, but as they progressed they started to stand for other, more fundamental needs. At Claremont Road, which was to be demolished to make way for the M11 motorway link, the struggle increasingly came to be about protecting a whole way (or ways) of life. For many of the people who occupied the street throughout most of 1994, the issue was the 1994 Criminal Justice and Public Order Act which was an attack on non-mainstream ways of life. Claremont Road was a free space, a social focus for those who felt attacked by the legislation.

"The act of standing in front of a bulldozer is not merely practical it is deeply symbolic," says Sam of Reclaim the Streets. "The defiant protester is rejecting a system in which progress is measured by Gross National Product, where landscapes such as Twyford Down are sacrificed to this false economic growth in which there is freedom for motor manufacturers, oil companies and other global corporations to make profits regardless of the environmental and social consequences."

Whatley Quarry, December 1995
Earth First! groups gather from around the country to protest against this ever expanding source of road stone. Work stops for one day, many activists arrested.

Photo: Nick Cobbing

M11, East London, February 1995
Invasion of one of the work compounds
on the route of the M11 link road

Photo: Nick Cobbing

Even for the local, more mainstream campaigners, once they became involved the issue of roads was not straightforward. Not wanting something in your backyard means examining how it got there. Gradually people began to look at the wider picture, from the specific to the general, from county council to Westminster.

"I've been covering these campaigns and noticed how people move from the specific to the general, they start from NIMBYism and insecurity and end up in passion," says the photographer Adrian Harris. "They begin to look further than the immediate problem and to question things at the level of the police, society and even democracy itself."

One of those is Lucy Ann Palmer of Wells in Somerset: "I used to think that I was living in a democracy, but now, after an extended campaign which involved many other people, as well as me, in a bid to stop the authorities from building an unnecessary road at Solsbury Hill, I am forced to question the whole concept of democracy."

For many, involvement in anti-roads campaigns has changed their life, or become a way of life. Some have even been arrested, got a criminal record, spent time in jail.

"I am one of those still being sued by the Department of Transport," says Chris Gillham of the Twyford Down Association. "I have spent a lot of money; my family life has been unsettled by the threats over it. I even broke my arm, foolishly, pointlessly on Twyford Down. I can hardly bear to look at the place and find myself taking detours to avoid it. Yet I am grateful.

"What is there to be grateful about? There is certainly consolation in knowing that Twyford Down has set in train a process that promises change. But the reason I am grateful is that Twyford Down has changed my way of thinking and has given me a feeling of self-worth that I never had before. It has brought me a new companionship, a sense of trust in people and a feeling of community. And all of this with a sharp edge of excitement."

RECLAIM THE STREETS' M41 OCCUPATION IN WEST LONDON, JULY 1996

Ian, a Reclaim the Streets activist

"How an action generally evolves is that if somebody has a strong idea they put it forward and we consider if it will work. If enough people agree then we all meet and find out what our commitments and roles will be. A closed core group then forms to keep the location secret.

Publicity is always a critical part of an event. In this case we put out a flier earlier in the year specifically for performers, bands, sound systems – anyone who wanted to participate in more than just a passive way. That sent out the idea that we were planning something and we fixed a date, 23 July.

The plan was broken down into two main parts: the crowd and the sound system. We flyposted three weeks before the event. The meeting point was Liverpool Street station and around 3,000 people turned up. Ten people knew where the action was going to be; six facilitators followed each of them and directed the crowd. We took the people to Shepherd's Bush on the underground – it took eight tube loads.

We were planning to get on the motorway there but the police had beat us to it and were blocking the way. It looked as if the action was doomed but we managed to find two alternative routes (despite our mobile phones breaking down which hampered the decision-making) and took a large part of the crowd round the block, behind police lines and on to the motorway. Some had already reached it by going through some back streets.

Meanwhile the sound system, which was waiting a few hundred yards down the motorway in two trucks, had been told everything was off. But luckily they decided to go for it anyway, with two cars behind that staged a crash, blocking the carriageway. The police tried to arrest the people in the trucks but by now the crowd was surging ahead so the police beat a hasty retreat.

A feature was the skirts – wooden frames in which a person would stand on a platform, looking like a giant in Elizabethan costume. Most of the time they were just wheeled up and down the motorway with the person on top scattering glitter like at a carnival. Then we stopped them near the sound system to hide the noise and someone got in the bottom of each and started digging holes in the tarmac with petrol-driven road hammers.

Actually, the holes weren't that big. But there were quite a few of them."

Tinker's Bubble, Little Norton, Somerset
The residents are fighting a planning system which makes very little accommodation for "low impact" settlements like theirs in Somerset

Photo: Nick Cobbing

"*Land is the fundamental issue, it is about us wanting to live our way of life on our planet but people are saying 'sorry but this planet ain't yours, this planet is ours and we control it'. The land issue is about sanctity: sanctity of property rights and sanctity of life.*"
Glen Jenkins, a founder of the Exodus Collective, a community housing project in Luton

Land and Housing

*"**This earth we will make whole**

So it can be common treasury for all"

The Diggers, 1649

In contrast to some other aspects of DIY Culture, actions connected with land rights and housing aren't just about protest, about saying "no" to what appals. They are about creating alternatives, setting an agenda – rather than reacting to someone else's. They are about control and independence, about sustainable living and rebuilding communities and individuals. This is one of the key areas of DIY and the one that is most driven by need, illustrating the difference between DIY and the more middle-class ideologically-driven movements of the 1960s.

Land is the underlying factor lurking beneath the surface of many "single issues" – from the countryside being destroyed, to the loss of public space in towns, homelessness, house-owners facing negative equity, the freedom to hold festivals, road building and the slow death of many town centres. Access to land for living, providing food and recreation is an essential determinant of our quality of life, yet about 75 per cent of British land is owned by 1 per cent of its people. This imbalance is the structure upon which our society has been built. But cracks are appearing and questions are being asked about how this structure stays stable and who is supporting it.

Decisions abut land use are rarely in the hands of ordinary people, but lie with big business and the Government. At the same time, pressure on the land is increasing as the population grows and people demand new amenities like out-of-town shopping centres and golf courses. According to some estimates, every eight days one square mile of Britain disappears under building or tarmac. If current rates of development continue, 20 per cent of England will be urbanised by 2050. Britain now has 226 square miles of parking space, an area ten times the size of Southampton.

To some people, land is a commodity; to others it is something much purer and more basic, encompassing social, economic, environmental, political and historical issues.

"It is accepted that those in power can sell our woodlands and put 'Keep Out' notices on them. I find it strange," says Charles Denton, a campaigner for pensioners' rights. "I buried some of my friends in the Western Desert. We were supposed to be fighting for this country, but they can sell this country and we can do nothing about it."

Similar sentiments exist among younger generations: "The concept of land ownership is absurd. I mean how can you own something that was there before you and will be there after you?" says Jules, a traveller. "There is no common land left and that is the thing that annoys people the most, that all land is 'owned' by someone."

DIY Culture may be a product of the 1990s, but the efforts of many DIYers to reclaim land for public benefit have their roots in past struggles such as those of the Diggers, the branch of the Levellers who pioneered economic democracy in the 17th century. In defiance of the enclosures of common land by royalty and wealthy owners, the Diggers went to St George's Hill in Surrey to create a commune in which they could house and feed themselves.

The commune lasted several months before it was destroyed by the authorities. To celebrate the event, more than 300 years later, The Land is Ours movement re-enacted the occupation of St George's Hill, which is now a golf course and private estate.

Brazil 1994
Members of Movimento Sem Terra, the
land rights movement which is fighting
against the displacement of peasants
and indigenous people by mining, logging
and other industries

Photo: Christian Aid, G Featherstone

Surrey, Spring 1995
Planting a tree on St George's Hill
– site of the original Diggers actions
almost 350 years before – as part of
a Land is Ours occupation

Photo: Nick Cobbing

The Land is Ours was set up by George Monbiot of the Centre for Environmental Policy and Understanding at Green College, Oxford as a way of uniting green and social concerns. He was inspired by the struggles of native peoples for land in Brazil and could see the parallels in Britain.

Monbiot emphasises that his group hasn't invented the issue of land rights. "It really is there and the only reason that people haven't been able to see it is that it is so big," he says. "But as soon as you shine the light everybody can see. They say: 'Ah yes, that is why that superstore is being built when we didn't want a superstore there. That is why I have negative equity on my house. That is why I am not allowed to stop by the side of the road. That is why we are losing allotments to developers.'"

Anyone who is buying or renting a house is paying a whack of money to a building society, developer or landlord in a vicious circle of hugely inflated land values. Land prices dictate property prices, which determine what the land will be used for. A shopping centre will generate more revenue than low-cost housing, so it's obvious what any profit-conscious developer is going to do.

Keeping sites derelict or properties empty can be more profitable than housing people. Between 1990 and 1993, the number of empty properties rose by 12.5 per cent, according to Wasted Homes, a report by the Association of District Councils.

Yet this country has the second highest homeless figure in Europe (eight out of every 1,000 people) and invests the second lowest amount in housing (3.5 per cent of Gross Domestic Product). Sleeping rough in the streets of our major cities only represents one aspect of the housing crisis. The less visible ones are teenagers living in hostels, families squeezed into bed and breakfast accommodation, young people moving from the country because they can't afford housing in the area they grew up in, empty properties, repossessions and negative equity, unaffordable rents and lack of student digs.

Council housing used to be an option for many of these people but restrictions by Conservative governments between 1979 and 1997 prevented councils building homes. Housing associations have tried to bridge the gap but have failed. Britain needs between 90,000 and 120,000 new affordable homes every year, yet only 30,000 to 40,000 are being built, according to The Land is Ours. "Land and housing shouldn't be kept derelict as an investment," say Dave and Darna, squatters in Nottingham. "There should be laws against landlords who keep properties empty on purpose."

But there aren't. In London alone there are 5,600 acres of derelict land – the size of the Borough of Westminster. In response, The Land is Ours staged a mass occupation in 1996 of a site in Wandsworth, south London that had been left vacant for seven years.

Even the conservative Sunday Telegraph had some sympathy with the action: "They are of course, dismissed by angry councillors, their protest considered irrelevant, their presence a damned nuisance," said an editorial. "But they have a point when they claim to speak for all who are weary of inner-city dereliction and tracts of land that lie unused for years, despoiled by previous occupants."

The occupation lasted three months before people were evicted and the spirit lives on in the Gargoyle Wharf Action Group, a mixture of local residents and those involved in the occupation. The group aims to make sure future development of the site takes into account the local community's wishes, as has been the case at Coin Street on London's South Bank.

The Land is Ours occupation, Wandsworth, Summer 1996
Building a yurt, one of the many structures put up on formerly derelict land in Wandsworth, South London

Photo: Nick Cobbing

HOW THE LAND IS OURS OCCUPIED THE GUINNESS SITE IN WANDSWORTH, SUMMER 1996

Nick Harris site press officer

"Around 200 of us met on Sunday in Hammersmith We didn't know where we were going but had all our stuff with us, ready for a stay, and just got onto the buses that had been laid on.

When we got to the site we went in, looked around and met up about half an hour later to make some plans. The organisers had already decided on certain things, like where to build the communal building (the round house) but the rest was really up to us.

We set about unpacking vans with the building materials – all reclaimed stuff from skips and even some struts from a church that was being demolished. We also had several tons of mushroom compost to make vegetable beds.

About 100 people stayed for the week, the atmosphere was inspiring, the work tiring, but there was an amazing energy. There was a meeting every morning to decide what needed doing. Usually someone came up with an idea and then people just got on with it – like the guy who told us that there were more than 350 species

of plant on the site and he was worried that they were being trampled underfoot. He suggested building stone paths all around the site – so we did, everyone joined in.

Other things we did included: dropping leaflets locally to explain what we were up to, tidying up the site, building vegetable plots and painting banners. One guy made a beautiful mosaic on the river wall. We created a plan about how to use the site and incorporated the views of the locals, then had a symbolic handing over of a key to a member of the local community.

A lot of food had been collected in advance, but afterwards a lot of local people supplied food and money. There was Alex, who ran an organic food shop and delivery service in Camden, who used to drive down and give us his out-of-date stuff. And supermarkets gave us food they were throwing out.

There were yurts, caravans, tents and clapboard buildings. People were mostly sleeping in tents at first but then started to build their own homes. One guy covered his hut in 'For Sale' signs – there were pictures of him in all the papers."

The squatters' advisor
Jim Paton, who is "as old as I feel, which should be 51", is active in the Advisory Service for Squatters (ASS). He was born in Clydebank and has lived in London for the last 35 years. His life has been "pretty much shaped" around the issue of housing.

He first got involved in squatting when he became homeless in 1969, this led to contact with organisations such as the London Squatters Union and numerous high-profile occupations and demonstrations. In 1979 he joined the ASS, just when the centre was folding and many people thought squatting had come to an end. But the housing system hadn't stopped making people homeless and Jim was convinced a new wave of squatters would soon be filling the empties again – and he has been proved right.

Between 1982 and 1991 he worked for the Housing Action Centre, where he acquired a lot of knowledge about the complicated legalities of housing rights and squatting.

"The general consensus is that about 1 million homes are going to be needed in the next ten years, so the pressure for housing is intense. We will see more and more self-build sites appearing because people don't have any other options. The crisis around housing and land is getting increasingly desperate and official political channels offer no hope."

This direct action has precedents in recent history. After the Second World War, many of the troops returned to find that they and their families had nowhere to live. Not content to wait around until something was sorted out, they acted and on 8 May 1946 the biggest squat in British history began. In more than 10,000 places around the country, people occupied derelict army camps, bomb sites and empty buildings. They rebuilt their communities to their own specifications. Their actions led to changes in government policy and housed thousands of families who otherwise would have remained homeless.

Today, the homeless don't have as much political clout, so there doesn't seem to be such a pressing need to find a solution. "It is difficult to make housing a political issue because even though there might be lots of people homeless, serious housing problems still only affect a minority of people," says Jim Paton of the Advisory Service for Squatters. "Whereas an issue like roads affects everybody."

Mel Young, editor of the Scottish edition of The Big Issue agrees: "It is quite possible to live in a good area, where everybody is working, where everybody has a car and a TV. So they do not understand that other world of homelessness, they have no contact with it, and likewise the other world has no contact with them either."

Where and how you live is intrinsic to a sense of security and well-being. It is the basis from which to organise yourself, and apply for jobs. "It's difficult to get or keep work if you're known to be living in a hostel or the like because employers don't feel that you are dependable," according to Ken Loach, the director of Cathy Come Home the 1960s film that highlighted homelessness. "Even personal stability and relationships are threatened if you don't have a permanent base. It puts pressure everywhere," he wrote in an article in The Big Issue.

"And it's not only about having somewhere to live. You have to ensure that people can live in some dignity and share life that's valuable, that has space. Somewhere to plant flowers, somewhere to let the kids play without danger. It's more than just a roof over your head. It's part of a bigger picture."

Throughout the 1980s, the Government encouraged people to buy their own homes, including cheap deals for sitting tenants in council properties which further depleted the stock of affordable housing. But the collapse in the property market brought disaster. In 1994, 1.2 million families were trapped in negative equity and 0.3 million were in mortgage arrears. In 1995, almost 50,000 homes were repossessed.

"So many people have seen their lives completely changed and feel themselves powerless. The sort of people who thought they had a stake in society now realise they don't," says Jim Paton. "These are people who have bought their houses and are now in complete shit as a result."

People who are most affected by housing need are among the most vulnerable in society: 16-17 year olds who no longer qualify for income support; drug addicts and alcoholics whose problems are worsened by sleeping rough. There are up to 1,100 mentally ill people sleeping on the streets in London alone. Even the Department of the Environment, in a report on the homeless, acknowledged that 30 per cent of homelessness arises because parents, friends or relatives are no longer able or willing to provide accommodation; 29 per cent is due to a breakdown of a relationship with a partner; and 9 per cent is due to mortgage arrears.

Squatting is one answer to the problem. It is a typical DIY action and has always gone on, but only bubbles to the surface when people squat en masse as a form of social or political protest, such as the three-month occupation of the vacant Artillery Mansions in Westminster in 1994.

Yet for most squatters it is just a way to survive; about one third are homeless families. "There are more people living behind net curtains and clean windows than there are behind old blankets," says Jim Paton.

Unfortunately squatters are not tolerated, according to Steve Platt, former editor of the New Statesman and Society. They are accused of being selfish, scroungers, not willing to wait on council lists like everyone else. Recent governments have not accepted the claim that squatting results from social deprivation. "According to the Home Office, squatters are generally there by their own choice, moved by no more than self gratification or an unreadiness to respect other people's rights," says Ron Bailey, long-time squatters' leader responsible for numerous high-profile occupations in the 1970s such as the take-over of Centre Point in London.

"Yet all the available evidence shows that squatters are homeless people in desperate housing need, often with other social problems such as the need to escape violence or harassment."

The homeless group Justice? temporarily set up a squatters' estate agency in Brighton in an attempt to alleviate the housing problem and draw attention to it. They argued that squatting itself is not illegal, but forcing entry to a property is. They did not actually advocate occupying empty buildings; just told people where they were.

There are alternatives to squatting, such as reclaiming land and housing, making the most of what is there, taking charge of derelict buildings, setting up housing co-operatives, buying rural land and living a low-impact lifestyle. One new initiative is the Groundswell Project run by CHAR, the Housing Campaign for the Single Homeless, which aims to narrow the divide between self-help and those living on the streets; synthesising the energy and motivation of the former with the massive human resources of the latter. Eventually CHAR hopes to have a network of projects tackling homelessness at the local level.

The Big Issue aims to tackle homelessness by giving people a chance to help themselves. They get an income through selling the paper – breaking the no-address-no-job syndrome – and profits from the general interest magazine are ploughed back into the Big Issue Foundation which supports housing and training schemes.

DIYers have also squatted buildings with the idea of providing a focus for the community. In London, one of the most successful was the Cooltan Centre in Brixton which started in the summer of 1991 in a disused sun lotion factory.

"Originally it was trying to make use of empty buildings, putting on art exhibitions, parties, poetry, providing cheap food and a place to hang out," says Shane Collins, a green activist and one of the founders of the Cooltan Centre. "The bunch who squatted the building were primarily artists, then other people came along and brought in the politics."

Other groups, such as those in Cardiff and Edinburgh, followed the example. Many of the squatted buildings provided a focus for campaigns against the 1994 Criminal Justice and Public Order Act (CJA). There is a need for this type of unregulated

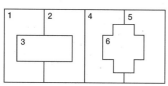

1	2	4	5
3		6	

1 Hotsfield, south Wales
Campaign against eviction

2 Kensington, October 1994
Action by SQUASH (SQuatters
Action for Secure Homes)
against the new squatting
laws in the CJA

3 Charing Cross Road, London
Homeless man

4 'The Grange', Norfolk
A rural squat

5 Cool Tan Arts Centre
South London
The front garden
of this licensed urban
squat in Brixton

6 Haz Manor, Luton
Ruth and baby Lyle at
"Haz Manor", refurbished
by the Exodus collective

Photos: Nick Cobbing

**The campaigner against
open cast mines**

Steve Parry, who is in his forties, comes from a mining area in Nottinghamshire. He is a former general secretary of the National Union of Students "when the NUS was radical", was responsible for setting up Workers Against Racism and helped build support among students for the miners' strikes of the 1970s.

Steve has been an almost full-time political activist all his adult life and was involved in the 1992 fight against the wave of pit closures announced by Michael Heseltine who was then Industry Secretary. The campaign failed and one result was an increase in open cast mining which is cheaper to operate.

Steve saw a direct link between the environmental destruction caused by open cast and what was happening to the mining communities. In most cases there are local opposition groups to open cast mines and he set up a national information network to link them.

To bring home the issues to those who make the decisions, Steve and 60 colleagues broke into the grounds of Heseltine's mansion several times to hold picnics, dig holes and plant trees. They have also submitted a detailed planning application for an open cast mine on Heseltine's land which the county council are apparently treating seriously.

"Marches are really a waste of time, you have to take direct action that grabs people's imagination. We are at a watershed. Local communities are going to transform the political landscape here and elsewhere and the Establishment is quite frightened, they don't know how to react. Things are going to change: people just need to have patience."

community space, especially in cities where there are very few free places to go. "If you're unemployed with little money, the options are squeezed out," says Shane. "That is one of the reasons why these community centres have been popular. You can sit in a cafe, pay 30p for a cup of tea and just hang out and chat to people."

As meeting places, and often as campaign headquarters, they spark off a lot more, says Jim Paton. "They get people's confidence up and encourage them to take the initiative and squat for themselves, to open empty flats to live in."

They are not always welcomed by the police and local authorities who see them as hotbeds of potential anarchy. Eighteen people were arrested in 1994 during the heavy-handed eviction of occupants from the Unemployed Workers Centre in Edinburgh. The centre had been occupied for nine months after the Labour-controlled council withdrew funding because it was being used as a base for campaigners against the CJA. The building was then sold.

However, the open-door policy at most centres means they haven't always run smoothly. There can be hard drugs and violence and volunteers often end up doing the work that social services used to do. "We were taking in people who had been chucked out of mental institutions, drug addicts and so on," says Shane. "It was very energy-sapping and when a lot of people went off to the road campaigns, places like the Rainbow Centre in north London got taken over by people who couldn't take care of themselves, let alone anyone else."

But it doesn't have to be like that. One of the most successful DIY housing initiatives has been set up by Exodus, the Luton-based collective. Their first emphasis was on parties, bringing together a multi-racial force to tap into the need for a dancing space. Exodus then tackled the next problem: their housing needs. They squatted one building and were eventually given a derelict hospice by Luton council. They have now converted it into Haz Manor, a Housing Action Zone which provides homes and work for more than 30 people.

"We have solved our own housing problem," says Zoe, an Exodus resident. "Everyone should have the right to do the same."

Housing benefit gets paid to the residents directly, instead of to their landlords, so they can use it to renovate the building. They hope to buy it eventually and use the Housing Action Zone as a model for others to follow.

"This system is unique," says Glen Jenkins, one of the founders of Exodus. "Haz manor incites people to know that empowerment is not only a good thing, it is the best thing that they've ever felt. We all believe in God, not the God with the white beard who sits in the clouds judging, but a God that says to live a harmonic life, to honour the Earth by protecting it.

"The essence of spirituality is to do good to others, but this society is based on doing well by competing with others. What we are trying to do is re-establish what we call a godly way of life – a good way of life, a sharing and co-operative way of life."

Exodus runs by consensus, in an organic way. "The idea is: 'let it go wrong and then sort it out'," explains Glen. "It is quite costly in the short term, but in the long term it means you don't have to have rules." It is essentially a housing co-operative, based on a legal structure that has been used successfully for years by people on low incomes to buy land and housing collectively. Co-ops allow independence and provide good quality housing. The bottom line is that there is no individual profit.

"We are DIY because we don't rely on experts," explains Stuart, a finance worker and administrator for Radical Routes, a housing and loans co-op in Birmingham. "All the experts told us we were rubbish. When the original team wanted to set the whole thing up in 1986/87 they went to see someone quite senior in a National Housing Charity who said the scheme was impossible. But they decided to just go and do it and it worked.

"Ever since then we have had a distrust of experts. We rely on what we do ourselves. We are not in the grant and contract culture which you get in a lot of voluntary organisations. If you want to take control of your life you have to set things up yourself that aren't reliant on Government funding."

Radical Routes is involved in businesses, housing co-ops and ethical investment. It provides cheap loans to people who want to set up housing co-ops and helps people on the dole, who have very little money of their own, to get a house together.

The volunteer press officer
Nick Harris, 26, was a press contact for The Land Is Ours three-month occupation, in summer 1996, of the vacant site owned by Guinness breweries in Wandsworth south-west London. He is a writer and editor and was brought up in rural Norfolk.

He was attracted to The Land Is Ours because it focuses on proactive ideas rather than just protest. He started off by going to a couple of The Land Is Ours open meetings and attended "out of curiosity" the occupation of St George's Hill in Surrey. Nick participated in some of the planning meetings for Wandsworth and gradually got more involved.

The Wandsworth action evolved on its own as everyone got on and did their own thing: a lot of people putting in a massive amount of time and effort, and pulling together. As with any ground-breaking project, there were problems but Nick still feels the occupation achieved far more than he had expected.

"It was not the solution but it raised the issues; it made people think that maybe they could have a say in how land is developed. I don't think land should be just sat upon until someone can make a lot of money from it."

Sadie Bowens Holtsfield
Autumn 1995
Sadie is interviewed by reporters
on the day of the first attempted
evictions of three houses in the
south Wales chalet community

Photo: Nick Cobbing

Joy and Nuala, King's Hill
The 'King's Hill Collective' is a community
of bender dwellers in Somerset who own
their own land but are repeatedly refused
planning permission to build homes
on it, despite appeals to the high court

Photo: Nick Cobbing

**Teepee, at the Cantlin Stone
festival, Wales, August 1986**

Photo: Alan Lodge

The teepee resident

Brig Oubridge, a 45-year-old father
of two, has lived at the Teepee
Valley low-impact community in
Wales for nearly 20 years. Before
that he was squatting in London,
running a wholefood shop and a
squatters' cafe. His first involvement
with Teepee Valley was to take
a market stall there and when
he moved in he ran a community
shop for a couple of years.

He is currently pursuing several
court cases in an attempt to
establish the community's right
to live on its land. A former Green
Party activist, his other major
activity at the moment is organising
the annual Big Green Gathering,
a festival powered by alternative
technology. His dream is to
wander around the foothills
of the Himalayas.

*"Britain is a country where the
majority of people have been
deprived of any contact with or share
in the land. Most, in one way or
another, were driven off the land
in the industrial revolution. Now
the urban population is no longer
needed, it is quite possible for them
to live in the countryside but they
must be prepared to accept a
much lower economic standard
of living. It really is the only way
to be sustainable in global terms."*

Co-operative loans have been used informally for years by Asians and Afro-Caribbeans in Britain who have a tradition of pooling their savings. The resulting sum would either be used to buy a property which would be rented to those in need of housing or lent at low interest rates to members of the savings club. Money circulated within the community and did not go into banks or building societies which have often refused to lend to ethnic minorities. It has helped build black self-organisation and self-reliance.

Self organisation is evident in Holtsfield, south Wales, where 25 families have been fighting for the survival of their an idyllic community for the past five years after the owner of the land, Tim Jones, decided to sell it for redevelopment. He demanded £1 million for the land and started eviction procedures.

Holtsfield began as a collection of holiday homes built in the 1920s set away from the road in peaceful semi-woodland. During the Second World War some families fleeing the Blitz in Swansea came to the summer chalets for safety. Many never left and in the 1950s and 60s other people were drawn in.

The problem is that the chalets have no foundations, so they are classified by law as mobile homes which means the residents have far fewer rights than those in traditional dwellings. The community fought for the right to stay in their own homes and were joined by DIYers bringing non-violent direct action tactics fresh from open-cast mining and road protests.

"Next door are making lock-on pipes for us to chain ourselves to, but the woman in one of the houses which is immediately threatened, she just wants to get up and walk out peacefully after making her point," say Holtsfield residents Dunky and Jenny. "We are outraged and angry at the evictions. One man with power and money walking all over people who haven't. There is a grave injustice going on."

To be an alternative community means you are often open to unjust treatment by those in power. One such settlement is Tinkers Bubble in Somerset, a group of people who have decided to live a low-impact sustainable lifestyle.

They own the 14 acres of land they live on. It is not a romantic ideal, an experiment for city dwellers or a quaint children's farm:

it is a place where people live all year round, not always accompanied by sunshine, birdsong and the smell of fresh cut hay. They manage an orchard, have goats and pigs, live out of sight in benders and tepees and basically just want to be left alone.

Mike, one of the residents, explains that they are fighting for the right to buy their own land and live a minimalist lifestyle. "If you want to get married and bring up a family, you have to take out a mortgage which is going to cost you £60,000. Then you better not dare to do anything wrong because otherwise you will lose your job and then you will lose your house. It is debt culture," he says. "Rather than letting people go into debt they should be allowed to build their own accommodation."

Across Britain, other communities are quietly living this way – Tepee Valley in Wales, King's Hill in Somerset – to name a couple. Sometimes a friendly farmer donated the land, or someone chose to spend their savings on it, or an eccentric millionaire turned up. To the communities, it means complete freedom; living without restrictions, in a manner which they believe in, building new communities.

"In the last couple of years there has been a constant influx of people trying to escape urban violence and pollution," says Brig Oubridge, a long-standing resident of Tepee Valley, a 150 acre settlement which began in the mid-1970s. A third of the land is owned collectively through a number of trusts; the rest is owned individually by members of the community who bought it from local farmers.

About half the 80 adults and 40 children live in tepees, the rest in caravans, yurts, benders and even an African thatched roundhouse. Some have their own vegetable plots; others make a living through craft work. There are no regular meetings, it's very much a "do your own thing" kind of place, explains Brig, "but within the context of a close-knit community with an ecological ethos".

"The people over in Teepee Valley are actually happy," says C J Stone, a writer and documenter of alternative culture. "They have enough control over their lives, they share, they are living close to nature and to each other in a more simple rudimentary lifestyle."

But these simple and seemingly sensible wishes inadvertently challenge principles of land ownership and planning laws. As a result, DIY living often comes up against some fierce opposition and bureaucracy.

"Development restrictions mean that if you can afford to buy a bit of purely agricultural land, you can work it, but you are not allowed to live on it – not in a house, not in a shack, not in a caravan, not in a tent, not in a tree, not in an abandoned fox-hole, not even a sleeping bag under the stars," complains Simon Fairlie of Tinkers Bubble. "You have to buy or rent a house within the development area. But this is so absurdly expensive, no one can afford it on the meagre amount that can be earned off a small-holding, particularly when industrial farmers with a thousand acres or more are churning out subsidised produce for next to nothing – not to mention getting paid £100 per acre for leaving a proportion of their land untilled."

When a planning inspector in 1996 recommended three years trial planning permission for Tinker's Bubble, John Gummer, then Secretary of State for the Environment, personally intervened to quash it. He argued that permission would only encourage other applications which, if allowed, "would have a serious negative impact".

Yet under Agenda 21, which Britain signed at the Rio Earth Summitt in 1992, the Government made a commitment to "support the shelter efforts made by the urban and rural poor, the unemployed and the low-income groups, by adopting regulations to facilitate their access to land, finance and low-cost building materials." Relatively little progress has been made by the Government, local authorities and business, so activists are doing it themselves.

Since the mid-1980s, hundreds of people have taken to the road for a variety of reasons. "There is a lot of attraction to it. For some it is a chance to have a bit of control over their life, for some it is rebellion, some don't have anything else to do, I suppose," says Jules, who has been a traveller for over ten years. "For others, the rat race is such that there is no real prospect of a job without ending up working for some horrendous company."

Jules reckons travellers are real DIYers: "When you're out in the countryside you are so much more more responsible. All of the things you have to do are tasks in themselves. If you don't do it yourself, no-one else is going to do it for you. You make your own fortunes. Although the opportunities aren't that massive, you can survive off a small amount of money quite well and and avoid all the grief of big cities."

Many travellers are from military backgrounds, are adopted or have been fostered or in care, so they have moved around a lot. For them, travelling creates a surrogate family, a real community, explains Jules. "Community is something that doesn't really happen in mainstream society anymore. All this empowerment of the individual has been at the cost of community.

"Travelling gives you the opportunity of having some renown in a small circle of people. Everyone knows each other and the festivals are the big meeting places. Your actions have value, especially in relation to other people, and I think that makes peoples' lives better."

There is, however, a lot of bad press and harassment from settled people. To quote then Prime Minister John Major at the 1993 Conservative Party Conference: "New age travellers: not in this age, not in any age." One of the results of this hostility was the Criminal Justice and Public Order Act which criminalised trespass in an attempt to smother this way of life.

"It's because it's such a very small country people have to fight quite hard for what they get, there is an attitude of almost jealousy," says Jules philosophically. "People say: 'I've worked so hard for what I've got, why the fuck should you get anything for free?'"

It is inevitable that there will be conflicts of interest over land use but these are exacerbated by the growing gulf in Britain between rich and poor. An exclusive club of developers, construction companies and Government ministers seems to be responsible for deciding where the priorities lie: whether land should be used for a supermarket, a football pitch, a road, new housing, a golf course or a conservation meadow.

SINCE THE MID-1980S, HUNDREDS OF PEOPLE HAVE TAKEN TO THE ROAD

Travellers Family
Tara, Mike and Coral in front
of their bus, with Sunshine in front

Photo: Nick Cobbing

George Monbiot of The Land is Ours reckons this lack of control over what happens to your neighbourhood robs people of a sense of identification of who they are and where they come from. People don't feel responsible for where they live.

"Few would deny that one of the causes of our most persistent social problems is a sense of hopelessness, the lack of meaning and purpose which results from the loss of belonging," he says. "One of the major components of belonging is our ability to identify with a place. This identification requires, above all else, a stake in our surroundings."

Alienation from the countryside, however, is just as consequential, he says. "When asked to think of Britain, many people think of our ancient, closely-managed rural landscape. The extent to which we see the nation as ours, rather than someone else's, determines the extent to which we are prepared to exert ourselves for it."

Northamptonshire, September 1995
Sixty environmental and trade union activists break into the grounds of a mansion owned by then Deputy Prime Minister, Michael Heseltine, to highlight the damage caused by open cast mining

Photo: Alex MacNaughton

The right of access to the countryside was a major force behind the founding of the Ramblers Association in 1935, following high-profile actions such as the famous Kinder Scout mass trespasses. They continue to campaign for improved access through lobbying and mass actions such as a recent invasion of an area of Pennine Moor which had been restricted to fee-paying grouse shooters. They have opened hundreds of paths that have been unlawfully obstructed by landowners and aim to make sure the land is available to all.

"Where you are walking is often an ancient footpath where people have walked for tens of thousands of years. Areas that are part of our heritage," says David Beskin, assistant secretary of the Ramblers Association. "i was walking a couple of days ago on an old Roman road in the Cheviots, past an Iron Age fort, and there was this historical perspective. There is a sense of freedom, tradition and continuity."

PASSTRESPASS

Selar, South Wales, February 1996
Locals opposed to Celtic Energy's
plans for an open cast mine at Selar
try to gain access to the site during
the eviction of protesters

Photo: Andrew Testa

This is one of the reasons why land rights underpin so many other campaigns, such as that against the M8 in the Pollok area of Glasgow. It's not just that the road is destructive and unwanted, but that it will destroy a precious local park that was given to the people in 1939 by Sir John Sterling Maxwell.

"It was so the people could have green space and enjoy what the aristocrats had enjoyed," says Alain, a Pollok resident. "It is one of the three biggest green belts in Europe. Scottish people have had land stolen from them for hundreds of years. It's just happening all over again – this time for the car. This shouldn't be built upon, it is our land, it belongs to us, it is our heritage."

The environment is often tied in with social implications, as at Selar, in Wales, the site of protests in 1995 and 1996 against the development of an open cast coal mine, by the private company Celtic Energy, which would destroythe valley. Selar has had its traditional underground mines closed and the protest is a tangle of political, social and economic concerns that have resulted in a network of alliances being created. Protesters against the destruction of land found common cause with people fighting for jobs and their village.

The DIYers went to Selar to occupy the land earmarked for the mine and found a strong local campaign. "Because it was something that really affected them, the community came together," says Nick of Swansea Freedom Network. "They had something I have never seen – community spirit. It was great to see them rallying round the site; the kids were coming up and wanted to know how to climb trees.

"It was a bit of a novelty to start with and that is what I thought the interest was from. But then talking to them there was a real passion, a real respect for us coming to help their community. It was a feeling of taking things into your own hands – not just individuals but the community. The process would be nothing without that village."

But the differences in backgrounds and culture did create some scary moments, like when the activists went into the local pub for the first time. "We were all scruffy-looking, wet-behind-the-ears English lads," says Nick. "There was this silence, then a big fucking cheer and we got bought drinks and we struck up this great conversation. It was such a relief."

The growing numbers of campaigns around the country against open cast mines have brought together ravers, squatters, miners and environmentalists who recognise that working together can be more effective than solo operations. Environmental concern isn't new to mining communities, points out Steve Parry of the Open Cast Mines Campaign. "Miners have always valued the green environment because of the time they have spent underground. They have a natural affinity with the earth," he says. "Mining communities have always been involved in social and political issues. There has always been a radical tradition of dissent and self help."

DIYers and commentators are particularly excited by the new alliances that are being formed: "Like when we dug up Heseltine's garden. There were a load of people: Leeds Earth First, Hunt Sabs, miners and ex-miners from Barnsley and Wakefield who call everyone 'comrade' and Anne Scargill," says Nick from Swansea Freedom Network.

He thinks the potential breadth of these campaigns is really important. "In the no live exports and road struggles there are various links being built within the twee middle classes but the open cast campaign is making links with people who have backgrounds from the unions and other working class struggles," he points out. "These are links that we haven't built yet and it is time we did."

Margate
Protesters arrested during
animal rights demo

Photo: David Hoffman

Our basic rights and liberties

"Taking direct action is a good feeling – a great feeling – because you are with other people like you. This is the first one I've ever done. There needs to be more people like myself to go against what the authorities are doing because they just aren't recognising the rights of the disabled."

Terry Bennett, member of Derbyshire Coalition for Disabled People

"Pensioners go on the warpath" screamed a headline in the Leicester Mercury in early 1996. "Militant pensioners in Leicester are threatening to block off roads and occupy buildings in a battle for a higher pension," said the article. "Ernie Hallett, East Midlands chairman of the Pensioners' Rights Campaign said: 'Petitions and lobbying are no longer enough. The Government will not listen. We have to move towards the idea of direct action, such as blocking roads and occupying buildings.'"

What's come over them? Elderly people, who should be taking it easy, playing a game of bowls or tending the rhododendron bushes, considering the use of civil disobedience as their main lobbying tool? Whatever happened to polite letters and the odd genteel word with the local MP? They've been ignored, that's what happened to them and now pensioners, like many other groups in society, are finding that you have to fight for what were once considered the basic necessities of life.

Since the Second World War and the creation of the welfare state, people came to take for granted facilities like high-quality health care, good education, decent housing, being able to grow old in comfort and dignity, access to employment and training, and adequate state benefits. However, the Conservative Government came to power in 1979 on a platform of privatising many public services and then made steady progress towards that goal over the next 18 years. For a while they got away with it; but as the decimation of the health, education, housing and social security systems has become apparent, campaigns sprung up to try to stop the rot.

Pensioners, led by long-time activists like former transport union leader Jack Jones, are a case in point. "We believe that retired people are no different to anyone else; except that they have lived longer and have a fund of wisdom and knowledge," says Charles Denton, chair of the Northwest Pensioners Rights Campaign. "However, they bear the injustice of having the meanest pensions and lowest conditions of working class pensioners in industrial Europe."

What is interesting is that these groups are not asking nicely for the Government to throw out a few crumbs of comfort, they are demanding what they see as their due. This is creating a powerful crossover between movements for social justice, human rights and civil liberties.

The Conservative Government's assault on civil liberties was brought home to trade unionists like miners and printers who felt the full weight of some of Britain's increasingly repressive workplace and public order legislation when they went on strike against job losses in the 1980s and 90s. These same laws were used against travellers, hunt saboteurs and people demonstrating against injustices such as the poll tax, the treatment of minority groups and unwanted roads. Thousands of normally law-abiding citizens have been arrested and criminalised.

The Conservative Government's poor record on human rights emerged when impoverished groups, such as ethnic minorities and disabled people, looked at the causes of their poverty and found that in many cases they stemmed from the failure of the British state to protect them from discrimination. Britain has been hauled before the European Court of Human Rights on numerous

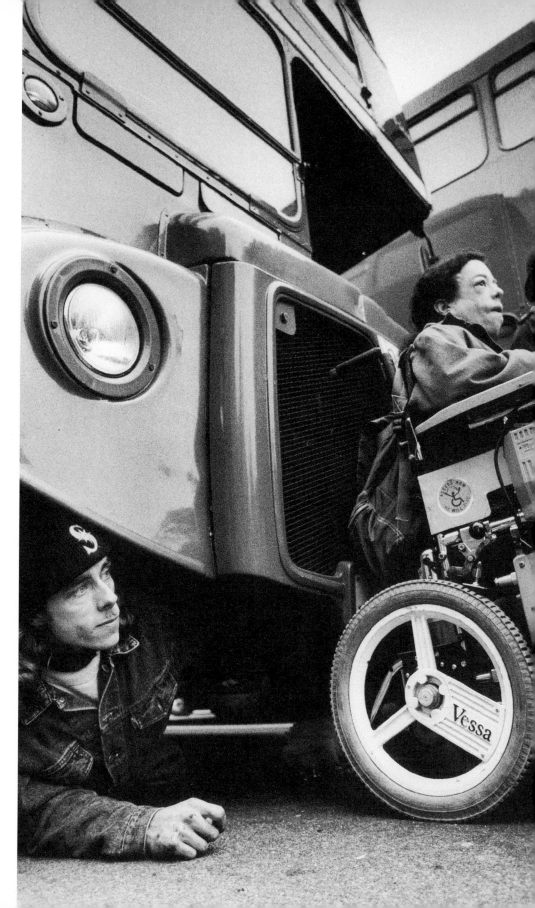

Westminster Bridge, London
Both DAN and Incapacity Action block buses and traffic to highlight lack of access to public transport for disabled people

Photo: Nick Cobbing

The pensioners' voice
Charles Denton, a carpenter by trade, is a 75-year-old activist in the Pensioners' Rights Campaign. He was born in Middlesbrough and served in the Eighth Army in the Second World War.

He has been an active trades union council delegate since 1948 in Middlesbrough and Skelmersdale and led local campaigns against job losses. Charles was treasurer of the miners support committee during the 1984/85 strike.

Now a grandfather, he is still an active trades council delegate. Since retirement he has become involved in the pensioners' movement, trying to defend local communities and forge links between the generations.

"If I was a stronger man, a fitter man, a younger man, I'd be down there with the roads protesters at Newbury and elsewhere. But really my struggle is here locally. They're doing away with our town centre and I'm trying to motivate people to say 'No' we're not going to permit you to sell the land."

occasions for its treatment of lesbians and gay men, asylum seekers, and IRA prisoners and suspects in Northern Ireland.

And where's the social justice in a Government that turned mentally ill people out on to the streets under the banner of "care in the community" and that allows thousands of pensioners to die each winter because they cannot afford to heat their homes properly?

The Labour Government came into power in May 1997 promising to reverse some of the Tories' injustices – but by no means all. So the single issue groups are continuing their networking. Inspired by the direct action movements, some have adopted confrontational tactics, often using small groups to carry out imaginative stunts rather than mass demonstrations. Like many other aspects of DIY Culture, they had been frustrated by the lack of results achieved through letter-writing and lobbying. As justification for their actions, they cite the – by now – familiar list of reasons: a Government that can't or won't listen; channels for complaint that have silted up; and no-one in business or Government who is prepared to consider real alternatives to the status quo.

Many of these groups have one major thing in common: they are fighting to be accepted for what they are, not just for what they want or don't want. As Peter Hope of the Disabled Action Network puts it: "Being disabled is a much stronger reality than protesting against roads, because the road will come through or it won't; you can see something being resolved and other people know what you're on about because everyone uses a road. Disabled rights are a different matter because not only does society not see disabled people, they don't experience disabled people."

DAN, which campaigns for "Rights not Charity", supports disabled activists who want to tackle issues that affect their lives. The British Council of Organisations of Disabled People brings together all organisations run by disabled people and is DAN's main lobbying body. DAN started in 1992 in opposition to the ITV Telethon, which attempted to raise money for the disabled but portrayed people with disabilities as objects of pity. DAN has approximately 2,000 members nationwide and carries out one action a week on average. These have included an "eat-in"

outside a cafe in Camden, north London, which banned disabled customers and crawling to Parliament in May 1995 to lobby MPs when the Disabled People's Civil Rights Bill was yet again defeated.

"It's a question of civil liberties," says Terry Bennett of the Derbyshire Coalition for Disabled People. "All the time we are having things taken away and being discriminated against. The feeling of going for a job interview and the minute they see who you are you are out the door is very hurtful. What we are asking for is civil rights for disabled people, because one day these people in the hierarchy might find themselves in the same position."

Disabled demonstrators have caught the media eye with protests like those above and against major stores like Harrods which have restrictions on wheelchair access: they chained themselves to the luggage department and brought business to a standstill. They have also chained themselves to buses – often at great risk – to highlight poor facilities on public transport.

"The disability direct action groups are saying that they don't want to be told what they want by the traditional disability charities," explains Atiya Lockwood of the civil liberties pressure group Liberty. "That is why the British Council of Organisations of Disabled People was set up. It is saying 'we want to be involved in discussing what our rights are and what we should be entitled to. I suppose it is very much in the same way as the black movement progressed by pushing for black-led organisations.'"

Atiya points out that accessibility of transport for disabled people used to be regarded as an issue of charity rather than of rights – an attitude of "we need to look after these poor people". But this is changing fast, she thinks, thanks to a general awareness of what people should expect from a civilised society.

A similar sentiment exists among pensions activists. "There are a number of organisations in Britain, with varying attitudes to what should be done for pensioners," says Charles Denton. "We do not presume to question the useful service that these organisations perform… but the one thing that most of them have in common is the concept that 'Pensioners' are separated from society, to be 'looked after' in their declining years.

The lesbian activist
Marina Cronin, 19, is studying
English and has lived in London all
her life. She was still at school when
she joined the imaginative lesbian
and gay rights group OutRage! after
reading about it in the gay press
and seeing a poster for "The
Teenage Turn In", in which gay men
and women stood outside Charing
Cross police station and confessed
to under-age sex.

Marina got more involved when she
left school and now helps in the
office co-ordinating campaigns and
smaller actions, known as "zaps".
OutRage! has around 30 regular
activists and a database of more
than 1,000 contacts.

*"OutRage! was so suited to my
politics I stayed. We don't really feel
any connection with mainstream
politics because they've let us down
so many times."*

"Some of the older pensioners were all for lobbying, greeting
their Members of Parliament, whining and complaining. But
some of the more militant said: 'We've got to do more than
that, we've got to start to do the same as other organisations,
in particular the disabled rights groups who have actually
taken physical action.'"

In many areas of concern there are already well-established
pressure groups. In some cases they were once at the cutting
edge, but most have mellowed and are now principally concerned
with bringing in new laws and tackling problems at an institutional
level. The new direct action groups are a product of their time,
responding to the same problems but with more haste and
a new approach. Some see the traditional organisations as
being too "soft" or acting as charities with a preoccupation
with fundraising rather than pushing for basic rights.

For instance Stonewall and the Lesbian and Gay Christian
Movement lobby for lesbian and gay rights, but lesbian activist
Marina Cronin reckons the radical direct action group OutRage!
was set up out of frustration with these existing organisations.
"OutRage! was formed in May 1990 by a group of people who
felt the traditional methods were going too slowly," she explains.
"The gay rights movement as a whole has tried the nice polite
approach of lobbying and campaigning but it just doesn't
work; or if it works it is too slow and is never good enough."

Marina emphasises that anyone can join OutRage! "There are
teachers, janitors, journalists, actors, hairdressers, photographers,
the unemployed, company directors and nurses. People from
all walks of life and all ages. I'm 19, the oldest member is 64."

But what does direct action achieve that conventional letter
writing and press releases don't? Visibility for one thing; being
out there in the public eye and in the media with an immediate,
clear message.

"The audience can understand what you're after, they can see the
impossibility or the unfairness of a situation which they wouldn't
necessarily have had to think of before," explains one disabled
activist. "For instance, one of DAN's main ambitions is to end
the discrimination represented by inaccessible transport, so their
slogan was: 'to boldly go where all others have gone before'."

Church House,
November 1994
Outrage Demo
Photo: Steve Mayes

Marina Cronin reckons you have to be shocking and manipulate the media to get the public's attention. "But we don't operate for the benefit of the media or for self-publicity," she emphasises. "We are just trying to reach people's brains via the most accessible means – which happens to be the media.

"You always have to think of new ideas. When we were tackling hypocritical bishops on queer issues we would often interrupt them in cathedrals but eventually the media got bored with it – even though it was pretty radical for the bishop and the congregation concerned."

Pink Weekend, Soho, May 1994
Photo: Alex MacNaughton

The campaigner for a fairer world

Angie Zelter, 45, is a potter, gardener and a mother of two. She has lived in north Norfolk for 20 years and has been involved in anti-nuclear protests and various environmental and indigenous people's campaigns for almost as long.

She has been arrested and imprisoned numerous times, first at the Greenham Common women's peace camp in the early 1980s and most dramatically in Sarawak where she was a part of a small international delegation attempting to stop the destruction of rain forests which are home to the Penan tribe.

Angie is one of the Ploughshares Four who hit the headlines in July 1996 when a shock decision by Liverpool Crown Court cleared her and three other women of charges relating to damage they had caused to a British Aerospace Hawk jet that had been destined for Indonesia – even though they admitted vandalising the plane. The women had damaged the jet to highlight the fact that it would be used against the people of East Timor and the jury accepted that this was just cause.

"The ecosystem is suffering so badly that people have to get involved in direct action. The public have to act in their own interests because governments aren't acting to protect the rights of ordinary citizens, other species or the Earth itself. We must expose and dismantle corporate power. Our democratic rights to a sustainable and ethical way of life are being taken away by trans-national corporations. We must shift the power back to local communities."

Visibility is also important in breaking down traditional stereotypes: vulnerable and pitiable disabled people; butch and aggressive lesbians; old-fashioned and confused pensioners. Faced with the reality of active and imaginative protest, these preconceptions do not stand up. There are powerful images, such as a pensioner throwing 25 cardboard "pieces of silver" down on MPs from the public gallery in the House of Commons, or going into the Savoy and telling the diners that the price of their lunch was the equivalent of what a pensioner had to live on for a week.

One action by OutRage! was at Buckingham Palace's Christmas ball. The group claims about one third of the staff are gay but weren't allowed to invite their boyfriends. "So we dressed up in frocks and wigs, glitter and tinsel and had our own Christmas party at the gates as people were passing by in their limousines," says Marina. "That night we were on Newsnight talking about the homophobia of the Queen."

When 50 Lesbian Avengers went on a tour of London's West End on the seventh anniversary of Clause 28 (banning the 'promotion of homosexuality' in schools) they did several actions including a kiss-in by Rodin's The Kiss and a visit to the lingerie department of Marks and Spencer.

However it is important not to let the high-profile stunts overshadow the patient, background work being carried out by researchers and organisers in DIY groups and in the more established organisations. These efforts have gradually improved conditions and often provide a framework for how to improve civil rights and social justice in the longer term.

An example is the practical, stunt-free work by black organisations. The Newham Monitoring Project is a highly-respected self-help group set up in the 1980s to protect communities in east London against racist attacks. The NMP combines a physical presence, such as escorting the children of threatened families to and from school, with lobbying and legal work. A similar organisation, The Southall Monitoring Group, in west London, helped the Lawrence family lodge their private prosecution against the men suspected of murdering their son Stephen in a racist attack in 1993. The police had dropped the case because they said there was not enough evidence.

"If black people are going to be involved in anything they will identify with something that affects them as a black person, for instance anti-racism, black self-help groups or workers' associations," explains Marc Wadsworth, founder of the Anti-Racist Alliance and former leader of the Labour Party Black Section Movement. "Usually welfare is more important than politics: immigration problems, struggles at work, legal needs and representations. Politics is a middle class phenomenon because the middle classes have more free time. If you are working on a factory production line, or in a grinding hospital job, or on the buses or trains you don't have the time to get involved."

Or, as Helen Shaw of Inquest, which aims to stop deaths in custody, puts it: "Many black people are involved in grassroots action all the time. The same type of people who would be involved, for instance, in the roads protests are already active in issues that directly threaten their communities."

In many cases, concern and direct action about human rights and social justice stretches overseas. In January 1996 Angie Zelter, Joanna Wilson, Andrea Needham and Lotta Kronlid cut the fence of Warton, a British Aerospace factory near Preston, in Lancashire, crowbarred their way into a hangar and, using hammers, caused £1.5 million of damage to one of 24 Hawk fighter jets destined for Indonesia. They vandalised the jet because they were sure it would be used against the people of the Indonesian colony of East Timor where 200,000 people – a third of the population – have been killed since Indonesia invaded it in 1975.

In 1969, David Oluwale's body was found in the River Aire in Leeds. Two policemen were found guilty of assaulting him

This is the only time police officers have been convicted over black deaths

After they had caused the damage, the women called British Aerospace's security guards who removed them from the site. A week later they were arrested and charged with conspiracy to commit criminal damage and criminal damage. The women spent six months in Risley remand prison before their trial in July 1996 at which they admitted breaking into the plant and vandalising the jet but said they had "lawful excuse" because its export would flout repeated United Nations condemnations of Indonesian repression of the people of East Timor. The jury agreed and cleared the women of all charges by a majority of ten to two.

The action at the British Aerospace plant was part of the anti-arms trade Ploughshares Movement which has carried out 70 civil disobedience actions worldwide. "The Hawks are part of Western arms propping up the regime of President Suharto in Indonesia," explains Angie Zelter. "It was one of the last chances we had before the planes would be shipped out."

Angie is a veteran of green and peace movement protests. She was a co-ordinator of the Snowball Campaign for Peace in the 1980s in which several thousand people were arrested for cutting the wire around United States missile bases in the UK and she was part of the women's peace camp at the Greenham Common nuclear missile base in Berkshire. She says the experience at Greenham was "empowering" – the description that many people give to direct action.

"It showed that ordinary women, without access to specialised information, can get to together and make a stand," she explains. "In contrast, some more established campaigning groups can be disempowering because they can be quite high-powered and full of 'experts' who make you feel that you can't possibly understand all the issues."

Greenham was an early example of the state's brutal response to DIY action. The women's camp, which was on common land, was frequently broken up by police, the tents and benders destroyed and the women roughly arrested. These harsh responses have intensified and have been legitimised by the Criminal Justice and Public Order Act 1994 which was brought in by a Conservative government but not opposed by the Labour leadership.

Anti Nazi League demo
Brockwell Park, south London, May 1994

Photo: Alex MacNaughton

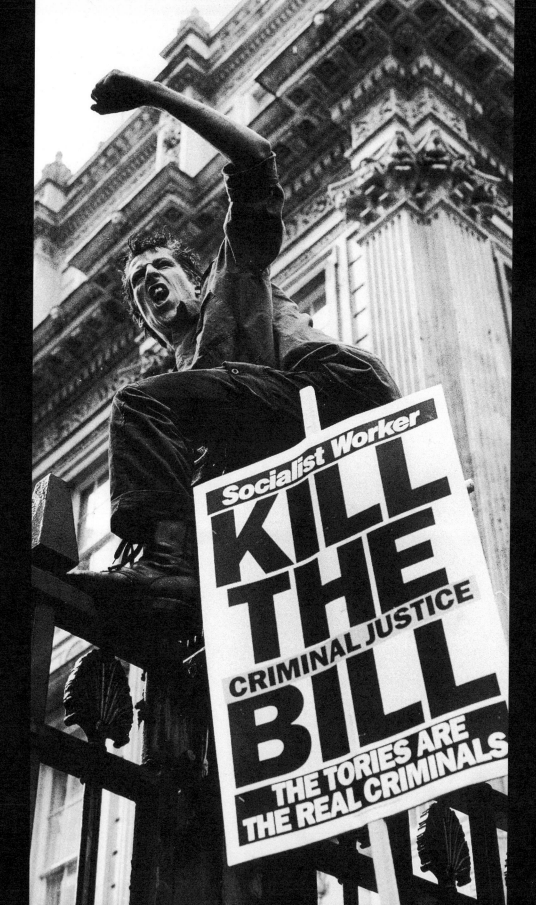

**Anti-Criminal Justice Bill
July, 1994**
Demonstrator on the gates
of Downing Street

Photo: Alex MacNaughton

Direct action groups and the whole of DIY Culture have been targeted by the Act which contains specific new powers to restrict trespass and protest. It has touched people right across the board, from pensioners to gay rights activists, road protesters, football fans and peace protesters.

"The provisions in the Act dealing with restrictions on travellers, squatters and ravers, did target a specific group of people and a specific lifestyle," says Atiya Lockwood of Liberty. "It was very, very strongly argued that it was discrimination and a human rights issue, rather than just a case of not allowing people to travel, or not allowing young people to have parties.

"It was an easy way of blaming our current problems on an unpopular minority who were accused of scrounging off the social security, creating problems in the countryside by organising free parties and so on. But that is why it is a human rights issue because in a democracy you have to talk about protecting the rights of the minorities as well as obviously going with the majority view."

The government promoted the Criminal Justice Act in response to an increase in crime of more than 250 per cent between 1979 and 1994 – the biggest increase on record. However, as civil liberties experts such as John Wadham, General Secretary of Liberty, have pointed out the Act does very little to address the real issues behind rising crime. In fact, many provisions in the Act will increase the number of criminals by increasing the number of offences.

This is reinforced by Chief Constable David Wilmott of Greater Manchester Police. "Many of the problems presented by New Age Travellers, Ravers, hunt saboteurs, squatters and such

The main points of the Criminal Justice and Public Order Act:

- Sections 63-71 contain powers to control raves and festivals – events when music "wholly or partially characterised by the emission of a series of loud, repetitive beats" is played. Under these powers organisers of raves can be fined or imprisoned, police can seize equipment, establish a five-mile exclusion zone around the site, terminate outdoor festivals and arrest anyone refusing to leave.

- Section 68 makes it a criminal offence not to leave property after the landlord has gained an Interim Possession Order. This hastens the eviction process as squatters may face eviction without going through court procedures.

- Sections 68-71 introduce the new offences of aggravated trespass and holding or attending trespasser assemblies. Aggravated trespass is committed when a group of people are on land without the permission of the landowner, with the intention of disrupting the activities of others. With the potential to criminalise a wide range of protesters, these offences were widely recognised as a means to crack down on hunt sabs. These new laws can potentially criminalise anyone from walkers in the countryside to trade union pickets outside their workplace.

- Section 154 introduces a new crime of intentional harassment, alarm and distress provision. This means that if someone commits the offence of disorderly behaviour with the intention of alarming other people, he or she can be given a maximum sentence of six months in prison. This provision especially affects football fans, pickets and protest lines.

- Section 60 gives police powers to stop and search any vehicle or person, where the authorising officer has reasonable grounds for believing that serious incidents of violence may take place within the area.

- Sections 61, 62, 77, 78 and 80 effectively make it a crime for gypsies and other travellers to follow their way of life. The duty placed on local authorities in the Caravan Sites Act 1968 to provide adequate sites for travellers is abolished and it is now a criminal offence to camp without the permission of the local authority.

- The Act effectively abolishes the right to silence by allowing courts to draw inferences if a suspect has not answered questions put to them by the police.

- Sections 54 to 59 extend police powers to take samples of bodily tissue and allow the use of "reasonable force" in some circumstances for all recordable crimes. Information will stay on a national DNA database even if the person is subsequently not charged.

like cannot be solved by legislation alone, nor by police action following the enactment of such legislation," he says. "Many of these problems have much deeper roots and wider implications; it is for other agencies to play their part, as society seeks to address the more long-term solutions to the social problems which we all face."

There had been active protests against the Criminal Justice Bill becoming law. It was a great unifying force for those involved in DIY Culture and brought many more in. A rally held in Hyde Park in October 1994 was attended by 20,000 people and 2,000 police officers but ended in a street "battle". Organisers of the rally accused the police of a "heavy handed and provocative" operation. The police claimed that it was one of the worst riots they had experienced since the poll tax demonstrations of the 1980s.

However, it is unclear what the Criminal Justice Act has really achieved – even from the Conservative Government's point of view. "Shifting the legal goal posts is unlikely to deter people who are protesting over issues of profound personal conscience, like bloodsports or the destruction of the environment," says John Wadham, General Secretary of Liberty. "All the available evidence suggests that the Act has made people even more determined."

In fact the CJA seems to have focused DIY Culture, increased people's awareness and determination to carry on business as usual and made activities tighter, better organised, more undercover. "The CJA has almost made direct action respectable as a legitimate form of protest against the Government," claims Steve Thackeray of Leeds Earth First!

In the beginning, in terms of arrests and fines, the Act was not as bad as was feared. In the first week of September 1995, for instance, the Brighton-based group Justice? counted

The all-round DIYer
Steve Thackeray, 24, was at Birmingham University when he began to get "vague left wing, environmental leanings". He got involved in Third World First and its consumer boycotts over issues like Third World debt. By his third year he had occupied a bank and gone on a few demonstrations but it was all "fairly tame".

After graduating in 1994 he returned to his native Leeds where he helped Leeds Freedom Network campaign against the Criminal Justice Act. He went straight in at the deep end with his first action with the radical environmental group Earth First! – a mass trespass at Home Secretary Michael Howard's house in protest at the CJA. He then invaded a timber yard which was using mahogany, blocked roads with Reclaim the Streets and took part in an anti-car protest in York.

Steve is now a support worker for a disabled student at Staffordshire University and organises a play scheme in Ilkley that has "an unspoken DIY vibe" to it – as have lots of similar groups around the country, he reckons, although they wouldn't think of themselves in those terms. He has been a practising evangelical Christian since the age of 14.

"My Christianity makes me stand out in Earth First! circles because although most of them are spiritual, they are put off the institutionalised nature of the Church so they choose to be pagans."

EVEN MORE IMPORTANT THAN THE NUMBER OF ARRESTS, IS WHETHER THE ACT HAS AFFECTED OUR OVERALL MENTALITY. HAVE PEOPLE BEEN WARNED OFF DISSENT AND PROTEST? HAS IT PREVENTED ALTERNATIVE LIFESTYLES FROM FLOURISHING?

FREEDOM FOR LIFE

St Botolph's Shelter, London
Mentally ill homeless man

Photo: David Hoffman

424 arrests under the CJA since its inception: 154 hunt sabs, 70 road protesters, 45 football fans, 43 environmental activists, 38 animal export protesters, 35 peace campers, 14 tree defenders, 11 travellers, 10 ravers, 3 illegal gatherers and 1 druid. But fewer than 40 resulted in convictions.

"The law was so badly drafted that most of the specific charges were dropped because they weren't strong enough for the courts," says Atiya Lockwood.

However, since then the CJA has kicked in and tens of thousands of people have been arrested under it, according to Justice? At the Newbury bypass protests alone, the Act's provisions were used for more than 600 arrests out of the total of around 1,000 and many of these were convicted.

Even more important than the number of arrests, is whether the Act has affected our overall mentality. Have people been warned off dissent and protest? Has it prevented alternative lifestyles from flourishing? One thing is clear: travellers, their families and lifestyle have been the most seriously affected by the Act. They are caught in a Catch 22 situation, because the number of sites available to them has been reduced and camping illegally is now a criminal offence.

Since the CJA came into force in December 1994, the Friends, Families and Travellers support group (FFT) says there is evidence that the Act has been widely used to force travellers to move on. "Travellers seem to have no human rights at all," says Steve Staines, National Organiser of the FFT. "The hidden message is to go into mainstream housing or leave the country, or else face continual eviction, harassment and a lack of safe places to stay."

FFT believes that since the onset of the CJA several thousand travellers have moved abroad, mainly to Ireland (where the Garda estimate there are more than 900 British travellers), the South of France, Spain and Portugal. One of the few positive outcomes for those who stayed is that many county councils have now realised the need for site provision. Recently, eviction notices have been overturned in court by sympathetic judges who realise that forcing families on to the road is hardly solving a problem.

What of our future rights in this country? Are they being slowly chipped away? Do people mind or realise? Maybe not – until there is reason to use them and then it may be too late.

"Privacy, protest, family life, freedom of expression and assembly and freedom from discrimination shouldn't be treated as privileges which can be lightly swept away by the whim of government," says Liz Parratt, Campaigns Officer for Liberty. "They're fundamental rights in any reasonably civilised democratic society and are therefore enshrined in international law. And as so many have realised how few rights they can really lay claim to under our current arrangements, the most lasting achievement of the new public order legislation has been to boost support for a Bill of Rights."

In the United Kingdom we have a system of "negative rights" where theoretically we are allowed to do anything unless expressly forbidden to do so. This has created a range of legislation which states that we cannot do certain things, however there is no balancing legislation stating what we can do.

"If we had a Bill of Rights which was part of our domestic law, it would become part of not just the courts, but our culture," explains Atiya Lockwood. "If that was the case, debates in Parliament about the Criminal Justice Bill could have been according to Human Rights principles. Without these fundamental principles, what legislation gets passed just depends on the mood of the country at the time."

Whether or not we ever get a Bill of Rights, we will probably still have civil disobedience which has always been an essential tool of people fighting for human rights and social justice. It was particularly popular with the environmental and anti-nuclear movements in the 1980s and has had a resurgence in recent years as a way of exposing an authoritarian and uncaring state.

"Life is for living. It's no good sitting back and wringing our hands at injustice – no-one else is going to tackle it for us," says Angie Zelter. "And the great thing is, anyone can take part and if enough of us protest often enough, governments and big business have to listen. And in fact they should welcome us. Having ordinary people question those in power is an essential check of democracy."

Stonehenge, June 1982
Celebrating the summer solstice

Photo: Alan Lodge

Raves and festivals

"Wanting to dance all night – when there were hardly any places licensed for it and when the law was against having free parties – pushed people into doing things themselves which didn't comply with the law. That was the link."

Nick Saunders, founder of Neals Yard and author of E is for Ecstasy

Seasonal, religious and local celebrations have kept people in touch with each other through the centuries, providing a focus and identity, and mapping out the passage of the year. Dance has tended to be used at such gatherings to promote social harmony and a feeling of unity with the earth – an empathy with nature and a celebration of life itself.

Today's festivals, raves and free parties are a continuation of this tradition – it's just that now people dance to a different beat. Like many of our ancestors participating in summer solstice worship at Stonehenge or dancing round the village maypole, people involved in these modern forms of celebration believe they shouldn't be regulated or controlled, or exclude people who can't afford them.

From these sentiments grew the DIY music scene which operates beyond the usual barriers of profit. Its popularity has increased with the realisation that there is an alternative to paying through the nose to go to a trendy club or staying at home. A society that has 4 million people unemployed (ignore the Government's figure of less than 2 million – that's only those entitled to benefits) means that not everybody can, or wants to, pay upwards of £20 to go to an all-nighter or £60 for a weekend festival.

"DIY Culture has come about because there is no money," explains Debbie Staunton of United Systems, which networks and gives advice to people organising raves and festivals. "People need to have clothes, food and a roof over their heads, but they also need to communicate and to dance."

So groups of committed individuals, like Debbie, have come together to provide free or cheap parties for anybody to attend. Sound systems and thousands of people don't just arrive in the same place by chance, especially when a lot of work has to be done underground because the authorities don't approve. Somebody, somewhere is working very hard to ensure the parties go on.

"Small groups got themselves organised, built up sound systems and arranged parties with no commercial motive," writes Mary Anna Wright in The Rave-Scene in Britain: A Metaphor for Metanoia. "These people were doing it for themselves, providing people with the music they wanted to hear in a place that could stay open for as long as they wanted."

The parties have their own information systems, relying on the Internet, fanzines, word of mouth and generally the goodwill and determination of people that they should go ahead. Some have taken the parties and music one step further, to provide a whole lifestyle, proving it to be a viable alternative.

"Free parties are unauthorised gatherings – communities coming together, no 'them' controlling 'us'," explains Glenn Jenkins, one of the founders of the Exodus dance and housing collective in Luton. "A free party isn't put on by someone to profit from someone else. It is done for the love, the warmth, the smiling faces. It is the difference between inviting someone into your house for a cup of tea and charging them for it. It is the difference between feeling welcome and feeling exploited. We are building a community based on love, not exploitation."

Exodus describes itself as a self-help collective. It originated in the early 1990s from the desire of a group of young people to create their own entertainment because the music scene was becoming increasingly commercialised and excluding people through entrance fees and heavy security. Exodus then expanded through group activity, resources and energy. "We realised that other areas of our lives could be tackled in the same way, through self help," explains Glenn.

The visionary

Glenn Jenkins is a 33-year-old father of four who has lived in Luton all his life and is one of the founders of the Exodus dance and housing collective. On leaving school in 1979 he became a trainee train driver and quickly got active in the rail workers' union Aslef, eventually becoming assistant branch secretary. He was radicalised by the attacks on trade union rights by the Conservative government under Margaret Thatcher and by the rise in mortgage interest rates in the 1980s which forced thousands of people (including Glenn) out of their homes.

Glenn left the railways in 1987 when he saw how pre-privatisation changes were eroding safety standards and changing a public service into a commercial business. He was then forced into numerous non-unionised jobs and was quickly fired when he tried to claim basic workplace rights. When his first child was born in 1989 he started work at the Vauxhall motor plant but was sacked when he refused to load vehicles that were bound for apartheid South Africa.

A period of unemployment followed, during which he became attracted to the West Indian community because of their "We're not having it" attitude,

and moved from "beer culture to weed culture". Having no money, Glenn and his friends were pushed out of mainstream social activities such as pubs and clubs, so they started going to underground raves and Glenn was "blown away" by the willingness and communication between people. When there was a clampdown on these activities in the early 1990s, Exodus was born.

"We were all conscientious objectors to the mainstream way of doing things – competition, capitalism, individualisation, aggressiveness. We'd all experienced a kind of psychological smashing, a breaking of the spirit, through our experiences of being black or being in prison or being part of the miners' strikes. We looked at the United States and realised that our street hustler environment would drag us into a spiral of decline ending in crack and guns. We searched for an alternative, to create a caring culture.

"We were angry enough to be passionate, but spiritual enough not to be violent. We are ex-jugglers, ex-drug dealers, ex-bus drivers. A lot of exes; a lot of changed people. We are both proud and humbled to be part of it."

Exodus recognised dance culture as a useful tool for community regeneration. In many ways they represent the essence of DIY Culture: donations given by their partygoers have helped them set up their own housing project and a community farm.

"We started with a small red van – I was working as a window cleaner at the time," says Glenn. "We filled the van with speakers and went into the forests. A hundred and fifty people came to dance and we sent the bucket round for donations. That's how the sound system and other projects got going.

"This was June 5th 1992. By New Year's Eve of that same year we had 10,000 people."

Exodus's popularity has led to problems with the police: arrests, court cases and general hostility. But more than four years on, the collective is still going strong and the authorities are beginning to understand the local need for Exodus-style self help. The group is a true grassroots initiative: getting right in there, not just philosophising about what could be done but doing it – with success. In the first year Exodus was active, the crime rate in Luton dropped by 6 per cent. And in summer 1995, after the police tried to quell the rioting in Luton for three days with little success, Exodus just turned the music on.

"Martin Luther King said 'riots are the voice of the people' but we have beyond doubt proved that people prefer dancing to rioting," says Glenn.

There are other groups like Exodus – Sunnyside, Sativa, Hackney Homeless Festival, Deptford Free Festival, Desert Storm, Kingston Green Fair – organising parties and festivals, not for profit, but purely for the music and to bring people together.

"We were trying to get an arts co-operative together in a space in Bristol and Sunnyside was created," says Matt of Sunnyside. "We gave our first party in November 1993, to look for our own way forward, to do something together. Sunnyside is just a name that loads of people use to make things happen. There is no organisation, no structure, nothing like a company."

DIY music has come to mean much more than just dancing all night and getting off your head. "Festivals more than anything else question the notion of property," says the writer and Big Issue columnist CJ Stone. "There are vast acres of unused land that is really only kept for the rich and wealthy. Festivals challenge that notion of exclusivity."

Free festivals and raves are seen as meeting grounds where like-minded people can come together to celebrate their own particular way of life and culture. They are an exchange of ideas and information, creating an informal but resistant web across Britain and beyond.

"The whole point of festivals is that they are temporary autonomous zones… they are self-organising," says Debbie Staunton of United Systems. "Nobody is told where to go or what to do, everybody just does their own bit, meaning that they are much more forceful as citizens, they look after each other much more."

It isn't a minority activity: 30,000 people attended a central London May Day rally in 1994 to support the right to protest and go to free parties; 50,000 people were at Castlemorton in 1992, one of the biggest free festivals of all time.

However, some people weren't content with just going to occasional events and felt it made sense to stay together and live that lifestyle, so the "New Age Traveller" was born. "Between 1980 and 1983 there were between 100,000 and 250,000 people passing through Stonehenge; each year the a convoy waiting to leave the summer solstice event was double that of the previous year's," says Alan Lodge, a photographer who has helped set up welfare and legal advice services for festivals. "It was an exponential growth because it is a cheap thing to do if you are not working or on a low income."

But hostile, scaremongering coverage in much of the media has created the impression that festivals and free parties are centres of anarchy and crime a "motley collection of dog -on-a-string travellers, ravers, holidaymakers and hooligans determined to share, variously, their drugs, drink, music and defiance," wrote the journalist Ben MacIntyre in The Times .

The huge Castlemorton festival fueled Middle England's terror of the dreaded hippie convoy. As Mary Ann Wright puts it: "When would this filthy caravan of parasites, drug addicts, skinny dogs and children with poor potty training arrive on your doorstep? Why have the police not arrested and savagely beaten every last one of them? Would you let your daughter marry one of them?"

The travellers' friend
Alan Lodge, known as "Tash" to his friends, is a 43-year-old photographer who took many of the photos in this chapter. He lives in Nottingham and has been involved with travellers and festivals since the early 1970s – he became interested in them on leaving school. A former London ambulance worker, he often uses his medical training to treat people on the road and at events.

Alan has a philosophy of "If not you, who? If not now, when? If not here, where?". He regards festivals as experiments in how people might co-exist, without reference to those in authority, where instead of money, the participants are required to make a contribution through their skills, energy or time.

He feels that if you live an "alternative" life it is important to be self-reliant and so helped set up organisations such as Festival Aid, Festival Welfare Services and the Travellers Aid Trust which initially provided medical and welfare services and increasingly moved into dealing with arrests, offering legal advice and providing a point of contact for the authorities, often getting involved in negotiations and "trying to lower the temperature".

Alan started to take photos initially to gather evidence of heavy-handed police actions against festival-goers and travellers, such as widespread stop-and-search operations, and damage to and confiscation of vehicles. He supplied some of the pictures that helped bring a case for damages against Wiltshire Police following the infamous Battle of the Beanfield in June 1985 when a convoy of vehicles trying to get to Stonehenge for the annual summer solstice celebrations was ambushed by a force of 1,600 police in riot gear.

"Things have never been the same since the Beanfield. Travellers are continually harassed, free gatherings are now largely outlawed and most commercial events are subject to draconian licence conditions which are aimed at stopping them rather than enabling them to happen safely.

"Really the future doesn't hold much promise. Young people now don't know what we once had with the festival scene and therefore how much we have lost."

Right: Glastonbury CND festival, June 1986

Far right: Spiral Tribe at Castlemorton, May 1992

Photos: Alan Lodge

The ravers' contact

Debbie Staunton, aged 39, is a book-keeper and computer operator who lives in north west London with her two children aged 13 and eight. Her involvement in the dance scene stems from the music – particularly techno – which she sees as "a fundamental part of the human psyche" that brings men and women dancing together in an egalitarian way with no sexual undertones.

Debbie's life changed in 1990 when she went to one of the first parties organised by the Spiral Tribe sound system. It was in a squatted school house in Kilburn and the liberated atmosphere made her decide: "This is what I want to do." She first began running a party line when Spiral Tribe asked if they could use her number because theirs had been cut off. Hence the Advance Party was created, providing an information network for partygoers as well as helping people stage events. United Systems evolved from the Advance Party and works on similiar lines. Debbie became a central contact point.

She feels the scene has changed recently with people charging for events and becoming more cynical. There are very few free outdoors parties and the level of police persecution is intolerable, so people tend to go to mainland Europe for free festivals.

"This country is being starved in some sense. Freedom exists as a pile of sand in an upturned palm. When you squeeze that palm, the sand escapes between your fingers. We are being squeezd to death in this country, the system is being rigged against us. In the past, people who demonstrated were treated as political prisoners; now we are just criminals."

However, those involved in the party scene fiercely challenge this paranoia. "It is a fallacy that people left to their own devices will automatically want to commit crimes," insists Debbie Staunton. "Everybody has their own sense of right and wrong, of responsibility and morality."

It's true that there is drug-taking, but not everybody sees it in a negative light. "Apart from being nice for dancing, Ecstasy has a much more profound effect," says Nick Saunders. "It tends to open people up to a broader perspective and provides some sort of spiritual awareness. It is more expansive and liberating than alcohol; people feel less constrained and less afraid to do things. It takes people out of a confined view of where life is and what they should be doing."

"Have you ever been to a festival or a free party? No violence, no intimidation, just music and people doing what people do best: having a good time," says one party-goer. "You don't have to worry that someone is going to rob you or is going to turn round and smack a glass in your face, because it just doesn't happen like that."

On the whole there is much less crime and violence than at major organised events. "In 1994 there were more than 70 arrests at the Grand National, but they don't go and ban the Grand National," points out Matt of Sunnyside. "If we had 70 people arrested at one of our gatherings they would send the riot police in."

Civil liberties experts agree and have criticised the Government's attempt to criminalise DIY music events. "We don't ban football or rugby matches, motor or horse racing or large scale events such as the London Marathon simply because they might cause disruption," wrote Andrew Puddephatt, then General Secretary of Liberty, in autumn 1995. "We recognise that the upheaval caused by major public events is an acceptable price to pay for the cultural diversity of our lives. Yet the Government has chosen to penalise 'raves' in this way."

For the Conservative Government in the 1980s and 90s, New Age Travellers epitomised what was wrong with some sections of Britain's youth: social security scroungers who didn't subscribe to the money-dominated culture of the market economy and who were actually having fun without paying for it. So the Tories, in the shape of Home Secretary Michael Howard, brought in a new law, a large chunk of which was aimed at stopping people holding free parties.

Ladies and gentlemen, may we present clauses 63-71 of the 1994 Criminal Justice and Public Order Act which included the following strictures:

"A gathering on land in the open air (includes partly open to air) of (100) or more persons (whether or not trespassers) at which amplified music is played during the night.

"The music is defined as including 'sounds wholly or predominantly characterised by the emission of a succession of repetitive beats'.

"If two or more persons are preparing for such a gathering then a superintendent or above may direct via any constable that they and any others who turn up must leave the land and remove any vehicles or any other property. Failure to leave the land, once a direction has been given, or re-entry within seven days is a summary offence punishable by a maximum of three months imprisonment, or fine, or both and is arrestable without a warrant."

The unfairness of the Act – and its forerunner the Criminal Justice Bill – led to alliances between widely different groups where before there was little common ground. An early response was in October 1993 when the CJB was first proposed. "About 50 people, from travellers to DJs to squatters, met in a disused launderette and decided that the people who were being targeted by the police (ie us) had to take a stand and the Advance Party was born," says Trauma, a DJ. "It was a collaboration of ordinary people using the issues of free raves and their proposed outlawing to highlight the grievous abuse of civil liberties that was about to take place."

"The CJA brought together ravers, travellers, hunt sabs, road protestors," says Michelle Poole of the Advance Party. "They were all coming from different angles, all defending different issues but ultimately unified in their commitment to freedom of expression and the right to live and play how they like, without hurting anybody else."

These raves, festivals and arenas for social interaction have now become politicised and, thanks to the CJA, dancing has become a form of protest. "When it started with the warehouse parties eight years ago, people didn't have any political ideas at all," says Nick Saunders. "They were just out to have a good time regardless of the law. But if the law was going to prevent them, they were going to get round it and they succeeded."

SPOT THE DIFFERENCE

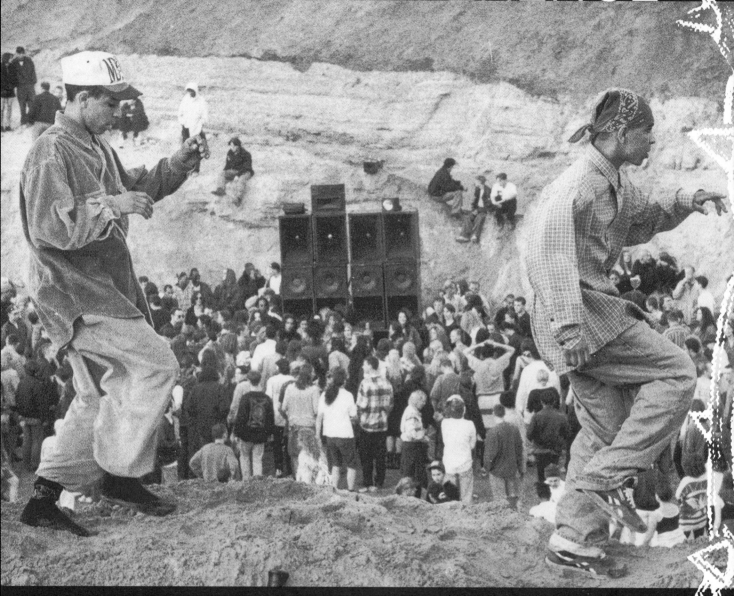

ILLEGAL THEY GIVE YOU UP TO THREE MONTHS INSIDE

Sand Quarry, outside Luton
Free outdoor party put on by
the Exodus Collective

Photo: Nick Cobbing

LEGAL YOU GIVE THEM UP TO £75

Glastonbury Greenpeace festival
June 1992

Photo: Alan Lodge

Stow Horse Fayre, Stow on Wolds,
Gloustershire, May 1989
Some people decided to stay
together between festivals

Photo: Alan Lodge

MOVE ON MOVE ON

Even some of the police, such as former Chief Superintendent Alan Marlowe of Bedfordshire, thought the Act was a mistake. "The police do not want to be in a position where there is a total blanket ban and opposition to raves of all forms. You could find yourself alienating people and having illegal events springing up," he says. "We have to acknowledge that raves are a fact of youth subculture at the present time."

However, many police have happily used the measures put at their disposal by the CJA – even against commerical events. Tribal Gathering, one of the biggest dance music sound systems, was forced to cancel a weekend event in April 1996, for which 25,000 people had bought £29 tickets, after Thames Valley Police complained about the likely traffic congestion. Paul Shurey, founder of the event, claimed at the time that the complaints were "part of a witch hunt to destroy dance music culture."

Another party, co-ordinated by the Advance Party, was broken up by riot police using tear gas. "Afterwards the driver of our vehicle was battered and arrested for supposedly throwing a bottle: the charges were later dropped," says one organiser. In response, many party-goers, organisers and travellers have headed for the Continent to escape the heat. Spiral Tribe spread Techno to France in 1993 and now people are enjoying "technivals" in Spain, Holland and Portugal.

However, there are gatherings in the UK and abroad, such as Kingston Green Fair and the Love Parade in Berlin, which prove that there can be co-operation with the authorities. "We should be working together with the local authorities, because local authorities aren't really an enemy, they are for the most part on our side," says Des Kaye one of the organisers of the Kingston Green Fair. "The future is in partnership. We have well-established community structures and they can be used to everyone's advantage."

Groups like United Systems and the raver's group Nottingham Right to Party intend to make sure free parties continue to happen – despite the CJA. They are determined to organise them and support those who want to go to them. "The attitudes of people have matured and the degree of dedication and, more importantly, organisation has rocketed as people have found themselves forced to become a whole load more serious about what it is they stand for," says Debbie of United Sound Systems. "Every weekend without fail, since the implementation of the Act, a huge party has gone on without interruption from the law. Sometimes one, sometimes two, sometimes seven sound systems."

However, the parties and the overall atmosphere has changed as a result of the CJA. "There was a time when settlers and travelling communities could meet together, share festivals, run stalls, sell things and be self-sustaining, enjoying the mutual exchange, knowing the differences and finding the common ground. Not so these days: the CJA has definitely seen to that," says Michelle of the Advance Party. So free festivals are a thing of the past? "As we know them probably yes. But where there is a will there is a way. Urban parties, whether reclaiming the streets or a cinema, are helping to keep that unity vibe alive."

United Systems' Debbie puts it more simply: "I can understand that people don't like our music, but tough. Just let us go and find somewhere secluded out of the way where we can play it."

Illustration: Paul Render

DIY Media

"Today, only the more powerful groups have access to and control over the media. However, the growth of the video recorder market and of satellite and cable technology has provided the opportunity to distribute video material without depending on broadcast television. My attitude is that if you don't like what you see on television, don't whinge, make it yourself."

Jamie Hartzell, co-founder of Undercurrents, the alternative video series

Alternative news networks and underground publications are not new. But recently, there has been a revival of strong and organised DIY media serving those involved in protests and eclectic lifestyles, as well as mainstream newspapers and broadcasters. The reason for the revival is the growth in DIY Culture with its dual need to publicise its protests and the associated issues to as wide an audience as possible, while keeping participants informed of what's going on.

Even though DIY Culture has had its share of exposure on television, radio and in the newspapers, news editors easily get bored. This means that the first wave of protests against issues like destructive road schemes, animal exports or infringements of civil rights will receive generous coverage, but later ones are given much less, if any, space, regardless of how important the arguments are. So DIYers are forced into ever more outrageous and daring exploits to attract the media's attention and bring the message home to the general public.

Playing to the mainstream media raises the unsettling question of how much of the eye-catching activity is genuine, inventive protest, and how much is there just to win the news editors' interest. At what point does the tail start wagging the donkey?

And activists have no control over what is eventually written or broadcast. The mainstream media reports in its own way, in its own time. It doesn't always have the resources, or the desire, to have its finger continually on the pulse. Even if protesters write the perfect press release, give an eloquent interview or supply their own video footage, there is no guarantee it won't be edited to suit the political agenda of a television station's or newspaper's proprietor.

"If the media are constantly saying that you are a bunch of long-haired hippies, it is not exactly very empowering for those involved," says Jamie Hartzell, co-founder of the Undercurrents alternative news videos. "But if you have your own media that is generating a positive image and putting across your message in the way that you are trying to put it across, then it is very strengthening for individual campaigns and the movement as a whole."

In response, a wide range of people have begun to produce and distribute the "news that isn't on the news". The aim is to give ordinary people a chance to have their say, instead of the usual diet of Government spokespersons and the editors' favourite pundits.

"The voice of the national media in Britain is not the representative voice of the nation, it is the distilled opinion of a select clique of mostly Oxbridge journos, who for some reason feel they have a monopoly on relevant social comment," observes Jim Carey, co-editor of Squall magazine. "Global media is now increasingly owned by a small number of media barons who, despite assurances to the contrary, directly influence the news agenda on the basis of their market intent. Squall is a serious attempt to provide a more socially relevant alternative and rejuvenate the independence and accuracy of British journalism."

DIY media ranges from fanzines to news videos, telephone trees to Internet sites. Those involved might be idealists but they certainly aren't luddites. They use technology to their advantage, allowing them to get information out quickly to a wide audience: after all, there's little point in taking action if nobody besides those doing it gets to know about it.

The DIY magazine

Squall magazine launched in 1992 as an A5 photocopied publication for squatters and homeless people. Over the next five years, it burgeoned into a 58 page tabloid magazine with an average readership of 35,000. Having developed a reputation for investigative reporting, the magazine widened its brief to include a multitude of subjects, populating the missing agenda in culture and politics.

The New Statesman described Squall as putting "the mainstream media to shame" and New Internationalist reported that the magazine was "fast beoming biblical for activists in Britain". The Squall team is made up entirely of volunteers which includes freelance journalists, photo-journalists and designers among its variety of committed personnel.

Squall's readership profile reflects the magazine's aspiration to "reach across the bridge", connecting those from different social backgrounds and fostering greater respect and community. Its diverse subscriber base now includes legal professionals, social workers, teachers, doctors, travellers, environmentalists and ravers.

"A large number of people are unhappy with the way the national news agenda is twisted so easily by spin doctors and corporate strategists," says co-editor Jim Carey. "However, rather than just be media critics touting a cutting diagnosis, we felt it was important to be active with the medicine. Necessity has bred ingenuity."

"These people are media-friendly, technology-literate and unencumbered by outdated ideological baggage," wrote Conor Foley, former policy officer of the civil liberties pressure group Liberty in the New Statesman and Society. "Anti-roads activists phone up the media to give interviews from the top of cranes while videoing the behaviour of police and private security guards swarming beneath them. The action footage is replayed at clubs and festivals or broadcast on the Internet across the world."

The explosion in DIY media stems partly from the fact that communications technology has got faster, cheaper and easier to use. "The flush of alternative videos that have been produced since the early 1990s wouldn't have happened without the camcorder," points out Tony Downmunt who has a long-term involvement in alternative video and is now part of the independent television production company APT Film and Video. "But for video and political movements to really find common cause and explode, they need to be primarily led by politics rather than technology."

DIY media is not above using the mainstream when appropriate, for example when somebody with a camcorder has gathered first-hand, fresh footage of a protest. This can then be passed to television news programmes who may broadcast the material, giving the protesters' viewpoint and stimulating debate – providing it is showing something new.

"All around me, people involved in direct action were using camcorders as a witness to police activity, and yet this incredibly powerful footage never got on the air," says Jamie Hartzell. "So I borrowed a camcorder and filmed an eviction at the No M11 campaign in Leytonstone. I was convinced the footage should be on the local news, so I called them, enthused them and they broadcast it."

There are opportunities and dangers in this approach, warns Tony Downmunt. "The fact is that TV news organisations are not funded enough to be able to cover things properly visually. So if you can offer them footage of something that is newsworthy and visually exciting, they'll buy it and it will get coverage for that particular campaign," he says. "What you don't get is any form of editorial control, so it is very compromised. You have to be aware that you are selling footage which may be used in a sensationalist way at best and at worst in an agenda which is anti the campaign."

The pressures that squeeze out alternatives from the mainstream media are not all political. Market forces shape how we are informed: the information that gets through is that which will get the highest ratings or the largest readership. DIY media is not affected by these pressures and that is why it is playing an increasingly important role in the world of information – by putting an oppositional, often minority voice that confronts those in power.

"No democracy can really work without a strong representation from all sides," says Jim Carey. "At present, corporate lobbies hold a disproportionate degree of representation in both media and politics. Democratic necessity demands that this situation is redressed."

DIY media isn't just aiming to preach to the converted, it is trying to get information out to people who wouldn't normally see the real footage of what goes on at protest sites; to act as a bridge to the mainstream, breaking down barriers and suspicion. "We're showing that direct action isn't this big, enveloping, anarchistic thing that is put across on TV; but that it is about ordinary people actually going out and doing it themselves," says the DIY weekly newsheet Schnews, produced by Justice? in Brighton.

"We live in a fractionalised society rather than a community-based one. A society where one ghetto has little experience of another except through the eyes of the usual media suspects," says Jim Carey. "Those who are into party politics seem worlds away from activists dangling off trees to save the countryside; while people forced to beg on the streets seem worlds away from those into the fashion and club scene. We want to celebrate diversity and foster an understanding of mutual need and value. Only in this way can community be restored. The likes of the Daily Mail with its 'Begggars earn £200 a week' nonsense are actively working against such a notion."

However, DIY media is not just about someone writing down their thoughts, reporting on some landlord's rent scam or using a camcorder to catch a policeman duffing up a protester. Getting the material printed or copied and then distributed is just as important. The major newsagent chains rarely stock alternative publications, so those producing DIY material have got to be very committed to getting it out and about. There are some organisations, such as AK Distribution, that are happy to

The McLibel Two

Helen Steel, age 31, is a former volunteer for campaigning organisations and has worked as a minibus driver for community groups and as a gardener. She now works in a pub, income £64 a week.

Helen was sued for libel, along with Dave Morris, by hamburger giant Mc Donald's over a pamphlet produced by London Greenpeace (an anarchist environmentalist group not connected with International Greenpeace). She has supported environmental issues since the age of 13, mostly fundraising for the big pressure groups. She became a vegetarian after a school visit to a slaughter house and edventually became a vegan. Helen has been involved in campaigns about animal rights, housing, the 1984/85 miners' strike, nuclear weapons, the poll tax, the power of multi-national corporations and the World Bank.

More recent activities include a mass trespass against the Criminal Justice Act, actions and occupations by Reclaim the Streets and The Land is Ours, and support for fast food distribution workers in Tottenham, north London, who fought back after being sacked for joining a union.

"Instead of everyone sharing the world's resources for the benefit of all, multi-nationals like McDonald's just want to use these resources to make profits for themselves. We have to fight back."

Dave Morris, age 43, left school at 18 and did voluntary work overseas before becoming a postman in north London for six years and being elected secretary of his trade union branch. Unemployed for most of the 1980s, he is now a single parent with a six-year-old son and lives off £70 a week benefit.

Before the McLibel case, Dave had years of involvement in neighbourhood housing and employment campaigns, anti-fascist activity, anarchist groups and opposition to nuclear energy.

He was particularly active in the anti-poll tax movements.

"I arrived on this planet before Mc Donald's and I intend to outlive them."

The DIY networker
Camilla Berens, now in her 30s, trained at the BBC and was a freelance journalist in the early 1990s. She got involved in the squatters' movement in south-east London and, inspired by that and frustrated by the lack of interest in alternative culture in the mainstream media, decided to start her own magazine, POD. The phrase "DIY Culture" came out of POD where the central message was; "If you want anything to happen, you have to do it yourself".

Camilla helped to start the Freedom Network, which co-ordinated campaigns against the Criminal Justice Act, and became its press officer, often appearing on television to put the anti-CJA case and helping to organise actions. She is now writing a book.

"There is a whole new generation who are very disillusioned with mainstream politics but are responding with their own DIY-style activities which centre on the three Cs: creativity, courage and cheek."

circulate alternative media, but these have a relatively limited reach and capacity. Unless you are connected to some kind of DIY network, you probably won't have seen a lot of the stuff mentioned here.

Another problem is getting sued when "telling it like it is" gets up the noses of those in power. Helen Steel and Dave Morris were taken to court by the fast food multi-national McDonald's over an innocuous-looking pamphlet produced by London Greenpeace in 1986 which claimed that the hamburger giant promotes unhealthy food, exploits its workers and causes environmental damage. McDonald's denied the allegations and in 1990 sued Helen and Dave for libel. The hearing began in 1994, and ended in December 1996 after 313 days in court, making it the longest libel trial in British history. Both sides called numerous expert witnesses. The trial is estimated to have cost McDonald's £10 million. Helen and Dave were denied legal aid so carried out their own defence

Although the trial has aided Helen and Dave's quest by highlighting aspects of McDonald's that Ronald would rather stay hidden and catalysed a huge support movement in more than 30 countries, Helen and Dave lost the case. The judge ruled, as this book was going to press, that they should pay the hamburger giant £60,000 in damages. It's no wonder DIYers are increasingly making use of the Internet.

The Internet was developed by the Pentagon in the United States as a non-hierarchical information network that would allow communication even if the centre (ie the Pentagon itself) was destroyed by an enemy. Perversely, this lateral structure makes it potentially one of the most powerful communications tools for campaigning groups and activists because it provides a fast, free flow of information for the cost of a local phone call (once you have a computer and modem).

The Internet enables people across the world to exchange ideas and information, such as details of the effects of a wide range of pollutants. The Net also provides a way to publish sensitive material anonymously. By the time a message has been sent via three different countries and numerous phone lines it is virtually untraceable. There is no censorship, no editorial control and the libel laws can't reach you the net is basically unregulated. A lot of the stories on the Internet would

Brixton, South London
March 1997
Mike runs the much
visited website Urban 75
from his bedroom

Photos: Sarah Chesworth

The State it's in

With media, politics and advertising merging ever more concentrically, there is no longer any border control between PR, news-spin and truth

Thouands of acres lie empty in our cities waiting for supermarkets, luxury flats and business parks. in may, 500 activists reclaimed a portion

HACKNEY POLICE RISK RIOT TO KILL JOY

FRONTLINE

AIR CAMPAIGNERS EXPOSE MANCHESTER HYPOCRISY

travellers parties protests animals reviews contacts

Earth First! Action Update

No.31 SEPTEMBER 96

30p

CARS COST THE EARTH

Special Branch attempt to infiltrate ploughshares

Festival of Resistance

Reclaim the Streets' biggest event this summer saw 10,000 people dancing on the M41

NO PROSECUTION FOR POLICE ASSUALT

'We need to start to build sustainable organisations to meet the sustained attacks that are coming our way soon.'

undercurrents

PROJECT LSD

WHOSE GONNA TELL YOUR KIDS ABOUT THE REAL DANGERS OF DRUGS - PROJECT LSD MIGHT

POLICE CLAMPDOWN ON RTS

the alternative news v

S ACTIVISTS HA E RECENT Y BEEN A ESTED

OVERTY KNOCKS

our're old or ill as well as poor, you dread the winter
d may not survive it. that's absolute poverty.

IT'S NOT THE DTI YOUR'RE FIGHTING IT'S THE GOVERNMENT. WHOEVER CONTROLS THE MEDIA, CONTROLS THE PEOPLE, RIGHT?

concept of a single issue group is now meaningless. We're making more and more links all the time.'

NEVERMIND THE BALLOT LET'S GO OUT THERE AND DO THINGS OURSELVES

TEN YEARS FOR ANIMAL RIGHTS ACTIVIST

MINISTERS VETO LOW IMPACT

THE LAND IS OURS
newsletter
a landrights campaign for Britain

WHEN A PRIME PIECE OF ARCHITECTURE WAS BEING ALLOWED TO DETERIOATE, SQUATTING ACTIVISTS MOVED IN

WHENEVER POLITICAL PROTEST BECOMES EFFECTIVE ENOUGH TO SIGNIFICANTLY REGISTER IT'S CONCERNS WITH BIG BUSINESS, MI5 AND THE ANTI-TERRORIST SQAD ARE GIVEN NEW POWERS TO INVESTIGATE

No. 13
Summer '96

SQUALL

Festival Eye

Out after curfew

- MI5 turn up the heat
- Raving in Bosnia
- Asylum seekers
- Poverty knocks
- Pirate radio

BYBURY NEWPASS

Travellers School Charity nets £17,000

CS GIVEN GO AHEAD DESPITE CONCERNS

WAKE UP! WAKE UP! THE WORLD IS STILL UNDER ATTACK!

SchNEWS 100
Published in Brighton by Justice?

OLICE VIOLENCE AFTER ISLAMIC FESTIVAL

STOP THE CLAMPDOWN! RECLAIM THE FUTURE!

Exodus defend community farm

Defending the environment is an ongoing battle for hearts and minds - and the environmentalists are winning

One of the sacked Liverpool
dockers uses a video camera to
record a protest outside the port

Photo: Nick Cobbing

not, or could not, be carried by mainstream media. The drawback is that there is no guarantee the material is true or accurate, but then that often applies to newspapers, television and radio.

Although at the moment "surfing" is a minority activity, things are changing as campaigners realise the impact of such a system. Cyber cafes and growing numbers of libraries and community centres provide facilities to allow those without their own computers and Internet connections to log on. Behind the scenes are enthusiasts like Mike who runs the much-visited DIY web site Urban75 from his bedroom in Brixton.

The Net is in many ways like a library with no filing system, so information is not easy to find. But as more DIY groups set up their own sites with links to other useful ones, the Net is becoming more accessible. "We are gradually moving away from the one-to-many type communication, to a many-to-many scenario," says Jonathan Bates, one of the designers of the Phreak web site. "Anyone can set up their own dissemination of information over the Internet; anyone can become a journalist. What is more, others can respond to your reports, creating a weight of opinion."

The Criminal Justice Act might have clamped down on the right to organise protests, but people are discovering other means to make sure people are connected and kept up to date. The whole range of alternative media enables people to plug into the latest actions and new legal territory – from tracking down the next free party to keeping abreast of Government policies. DIY media also stokes the fire, spreading ideas and motivation, both emotional and educational.

"The response has been like nothing I've ever seen," says Kevin of Conscious Cinema, a Brighton-based video collective which assembles recent footage from actions round the country. "The result after a show we did at Sussex University was three minibus loads of students going to the protests against the A34 bypass near Newbury. At the Green Party conference we had people coming up to us saying that they had been in tears by the end of it. They were all for going out and doing an action right then, at midnight."

DIY media may be a good thing, but it's important to understand that the power of the message and the apparent triumph of the people in the videos or newsletters doesn't excuse the rest of us from taking action, just because somebody else is doing something.

"In the stampede for representation, a caste of go-between mediators suppresses what collective politic could be developed and musters an automaton army to parade for the cameras," says one DIYer who wants to remain anonymous. "For instance Operation Emily, in which 20 women dressed up in Edwardian costumes and chained themselves to railings outside Parliament to re-enact the Suffragettes' direct action to win votes for women, was outnumbered by the watching journalists but it got as much media coverage as the May Day 1994 mass demonstration of 25,000 against the Criminal Justice Act."

Jamie Hartzell admits that Undercurrents is in danger of falling into the same passive bracket as TV, with viewers watching a video of protesters being beaten up by police or animals being ill treated, thinking "Well, that was awful" and then going to bed.

John Vidal, Environment Editor of the Guardian thinks DIYers should bear in mind that the media rarely changes people's point of view – just confirms it. "If DIY Culture was on the front of every newspaper, every day of the year, still nothing would happen. If you look at the front pages they are full of war, of health issues, of education issues: does anything change?" he points out.

"Yes, use the media, but what we are talking about is cultural change on a massive scale. I wouldn't try and change the world, I would just try and change how you live – that is real. What is so interesting about DIY Culture is that it has its own media and can feed itself."

South London, March 1997
Martin from Farm-A-Round
delivering his weekly organic veg

Photos: Sarah Chesworth

Community-based economics

"In the economic sphere, direct action is not about stopping a road, it is about creating livelihoods and the space for people to come together, to organise. Sustainable economics and direct action campaigning are two sides of the same coin."

Ed Mayo, director of the New Economics Foundation

While politicians and economists debate whether the welfare state can or should be preserved, the hard truth is that its edges are being whittled away: benefits are shrinking in real terms and social services for those in need are under ever-increasing pressure. In the meantime, while those same politicians and economists argue about the true level of unemployment, the reality is that for many people of all ages in the UK, there is very little likelihood of finding well-paid, secure and enjoyable work.

These are the days of part-time, short-term, poorly-paid jobs; of people moonlighting to supplement their inadequate dole or social security payments, or to top up low wages. The growth in the service sector means that for every convenience store, out-of-town shopping mall or 24-hour garage, their are numerous people working anti-social hours for a pittance.

One result of these trends is an increasing gulf in this country between rich and poor. According to a report by the Joseph Rowntree Foundation in 1995, between 1979 and 1992 the poorest tenth of the population saw their real incomes fall by 17 per cent while the richest tenth enjoyed a rise of 62 per cent. Today, 20 per cent of people in the UK live on incomes less than half the national average; in 1977, the figure was 6 per cent.

The root cause is the globalisation of the economy, which arose from technological advances and the deregulation of financial markets during the 1980s. This has allowed market forces to reign more freely over the international flow of trade and finance. Multinational companies, egged on by the financial institutions that are often their paymasters, can relatively easily shift production from one country to another in the interests of driving down costs and increasing productivity. The casualties are the workers – forced to compete for their own jobs – and the local businesses that supply the big conglomerates and their workforces.

All this is in the name of "progress" which has always been measured in terms of economic growth – Gross National Product (GNP). However, green and left-wing economists have over recent years developed a different set of measurements – the index of Sustainable Economic Welfare (SEW) – which includes unpaid work, income equality and environmental factors. This shows that although GNP per capita has increased in the UK since the 1950s, we are only slightly better off in terms of quality of life.

And, what the public may feel constitutes quality of life, is very different to the definition used by policy makers. According to a survey after the November 1995 Budget, by the New Economics Foundation and the Guardian, for the person in the street, quality of life meant: secure and fulfilling work, security, freedom from crime, a clean environment and a convivial community. Money in the pocket came way down the list, but this is what politicians and mainstream economists all focus on.

"There is no question that a free market system seems to be good at certain things, such as prices or a narrow sense of consumer choice," says Ed Mayo, director of the New Economics Foundation, which researches into and campaigns for sustainable development. "But there are other things that it is hopeless at: conviviality, social justice or sustainability."

The financial advisor
Stuart Field, age 31, works for the Birmingham-based housing and finance co-operative Radical Routes and is a computer consultant for another co-op. He first got interested in co-ops while at university and was so impressed that he ditched his PhD in computer studies to work in industry and on farms so he could repay his student loan and acquire relevant skills and financial experience to contribute to co-operative businesses.

Stuart's work with Mercury Provident, an ethical bank, enabled him to help Radical Routes launch their public ethical investment scheme which raised £30,000 of the co-op's total £300,000 in assets. He is constantly looking for new co-operative ideas and views co-ops as the "ultimate in stakeholding" because everyone who is seriously involved has equal rights and there is no one owner.

"In a world where there is so much abuse of power, the most damaging thing is when people say, as Margaret Thatcher did, that there is no alternative. This destroys people's efforts to create a better world. Showing that there is a practical alternative and that it works is the most positive thing you can do."

In conventional economics there is a term for the unemployed; they are classified as "economically inactive" and effectively have no role to play in the mainstream economy. Yet many unemployed (and employed) people are active in ways which cannot be measured or recorded in conventional ways. And when they try to enter the mainstream economy they are often blocked because of lack of training or experience, or resources to set up their own business.

All this has prompted many communities to turn to DIY alternatives like Local Economy Trading Systems (LETS), credit unions, co-operatives and neighbourhood food supply networks. These community economic schemes are proliferating, not to replace the conventional marketplace, but as part of a parallel, complementary economy.

"LETS and credit unions are not just cute ideas that happen to take off because people think they're nice, they spread because of their value system," says Ed Mayo. "They're rooted in social movements of people who are concerned with things like ecological sustainability, community, employment. These are actually common values that most people hold, that fit into their lives, not the value systems of the ivory towers of political power."

The need for alternative sources of finance, like credit unions, is clear when you look at the way conventional banks and building societies operate. Outside the Banking System, a study by the House of Commons Social Security Advisory Committee in 1994, found that one in five of the British population did not have a bank account. Out of these, 40 per cent were pensioners and 40 per cent had incomes of less than £150 a week (mostly single parents and the unemployed).

Many deprived areas of Britain have never had a local bank because the residents are seen as high risk and low priority. Now, even those areas deemed worthy of their own branch are losing them as the big banks and building societies close outlets in a bid to cut costs and stay competitive; and those few in poorer districts are the first to go. For example, 28 per cent of Birmingham's residents have no local access to banking services or are on the verge of losing them, and the situation is similar in Liverpool.

In any case, many bank services are not available to people who may have a bad credit history, too few savings or are unemployed – "untouchable" in banking terms. This is where credit unions can fill the gap. They are financial co-operatives offering cheap loans and encouraging regular saving to cover unexpected expenses, pay off debts or save up for a major purchase. In some areas, they may be the only financial alternative to loan sharks.

"One in six UK households is experiencing severe debt problems because of high interest rates and recession," says Liz Shephard of LETS UK. "An interest-free non-profit-making system has great appeal for them."

These forms of community banking cannot provide full financial facilities such as cheque books and credit cards. However, because they are run on a co-operative rather than profit basis, they can pay interest to savers and do not charge more than 1 per cent interest on any loan, which translates to an annual rate of 12.68 per cent. Compare that with an average bank loan (16-17 per cent a year), a credit card (25 per cent), or a store charge card (25-30 per cent).

"The people who use credit unions come from right across the social spectrum, but there are groups, particularly the poor, who don't have any other alternative," says Jim Dearlove, co-ordinator of the Birmingham Credit Union Development Agency, who sees the proliferation of community banking as a sign of the times. "Since the 1980s people have been hit financially. People who at one time would have been reasonably well off, are now having to cope with things like negative equity. They are much more vulnerable and insecure."

Credit unions have existed in Britain since the 1950s, but the number has shot up in recent years. In 1987 just 117 were registered; now there are more than 600 with around 170,000 members, assets of £65 million and loans amounting to £50 million. They can be based in a neighbourhood or at a workplace. The staff at Lloyds Bank have just formed one – the ultimate seal of approval. Observers reckon that every week a new union is registered.

However, this is still small fry compared with 66 million members in the United States and around 1 million (more than a quarter of the population) in Ireland. This community, or "micro", banking serves about 16 million people in the Third World.

The organic veg supplier
Nick McCordell, 26, runs Slipstream Organics, a box scheme in Cheltenham, which delivers supplies of organic fruit and vegetables to customers' homes. He started the scheme in June 1994 and has worked there full time ever since, with two staff.

Nick studied food marketing science at Sheffield City Polytechnic but had no green leanings. Those came during a work placement with a company that sold organic veg in Perthshire; Nick lived in a small country cottage and experienced a complete change from city hustle to a healthy lifestyle. After his degree he worked for organic farms supplying health food shops in Edinburgh but found that by the time the goods reached the shelves, they were out of the price range of ordinary people and already stale.

He attended a seminar run by the organic farming lobby group the Soil Association which described a successful box scheme in Exeter and Nick was inspired. With help from the Prince's Youth Business Trust, he set up Slipstream Organics which now supplies around 350 boxes a week, costing between £5 and £12 each, and the business is growing all the time.

"People who have no experience of organic vegetables are not interested in buying over-priced wilted lettuce or bendy carrots from health food stores or supermarkets. I thought that if I could get vegetables to customers in the same state as they came out of the ground, and for a reasonable price, then people would want to buy them."

A byproduct of community banking is that it can empower people because schemes are often run entirely by volunteers who act as cashiers, accountants and auditors, grant loans, chair meetings and organise committees. "Six years ago I helped set up a credit union for a group of local women," says Jim Dearlove. "Most of them had families and spent most of their time looking after other people. They hadn't had very many education opportunities, but were extremely competent in their own way.

"That group of women are now unrecognisable. When I first met them they had trouble seeing themselves as worthy people who had a contribution to make; now they have much more self confidence and belief in their ability to have an impact. Their household finances are in a much better state as well; their credit union has helped to smooth out the peaks and troughs and has given them a little more control over their financial affairs."

The Ely Estate on the outskirts of Cardiff has no banks and even if there were, they are unlikely to be interested in potential customers who cannot even afford to pay their water charges. So, if residents need money quickly their options are limited: ask the neighbours or a loan shark, or even turn to crime. Or rather these were the options before 1990 when a credit union was launched on the estate. Since then, each member pays in a small amount each week and if they keep up the regular payments, they become eligible for a low-interest loan. Every year members receive a dividend.

The only snag was that the very poor, those most likely to be in debt, had difficulty saving regularly. So the organisers in Ely created the debt redemption scheme which enables residents in trouble to have their debts bought by the union. The debt must be repaid, at an interest rate of 1 per cent per month, but at least it gives people a way out. The money from repayments is then used to buy other debts.

South Glamorgan County Council put in £3,000 to start the debt redemption scheme. The council saw it as an investment as it would hopefully prevent families sinking into a spiral of debt and crime and ending up as the responsibility of the social services department. A family that loses their home because they run up rent arrears, for example, would have to be put into bed and breakfast accommodation costing at least £200 a week; taking children into care costs about £600 a week.

The maximum debt buy-out is £500 and it only goes to people who are desperate – there is no cash for buying a new television. About 50 people have been helped so far and the vast majority have managed to pay back at least some of the loan.

These forms of financial self-organisation and reliance have been used informally for years by Asians and Afro-Caribbeans in Britain who were often denied access to mainstream banking services. And it seems that some things don't change: a report in November 1996 by the Building Societies Ombudsman, the Government's watchdog, uncovered widespread discrimination against black people who apply for loans or credit cards.

Business is another area where community-based initiatives are taking root. When a Co-op supermarket closed in the upper Afan valley in South Wales, the nearest shop was a 25-mile round trip away, so villagers got together and opened their own. The Gwynfi Community Co-op is the first co-operative retail society to be registered in Britain for nearly a century.

Several more community businesses are now up and running in the area. Glyncorrwg Ponds Co-operative has remodelled a local river into lakes for boating, fishing and tourism; Afan Community Transport runs a minibus service for an area lacking public transport.

Residents of a nearby town in Wales looked at their local economy and discovered that they were spending £250,000 a year on imported fuel. Their solution was to invest in a program of insulation to save energy, diverting some of the money that would have gone to the gas or electricity companies into local jobs.

Vegetable box schemes are a form of community-supported farming which evolved because many small-scale organic farmers were unable to meet the quality and quantity specified by supermarkets. A lot of their vegetables were rejected because they weren't the right shape, colour and size, although nutritionally they were as good if not better than the prettier, industrially-farmed equivalents. Meanwhile, shoppers found organic fruit and veg prohibitively expensive because organic farmers receive few of the European Union subsidies which go to the big farms.

Box schemes solve some of the problems by providing a direct link between organic farmers and consumers. There are now more than 250 box schemes. The biggest is Organic Roundabout in Birmingham (part of the Radical Routes Co-operative), which employs 12 people and distributes produce from more than 30 growers in Herefordshire to 1,000 homes in the West Midlands.

There are various types of scheme but the principle is the same: customers are supplied with organic vegetables that they can afford and which are grown nearby. The average cost for a 10 pound box of vegetables is around £5. "We are getting good food to people at a price they can afford and which they have some control over," explains Alan Brockman, an organic grower from Kent. Customers seem happy although some complain about a lack of variety, particularly in winter.

More ambitious still are Local Exchange Trading Systems (LETS) which have grown exponentially in the UK over the last few years from four schemes in 1990, to approximately 400 schemes today involving more than 40,000 people. LETS is a form of bartering that makes use of the skills and energy that exist in communities but that often have difficulty finding an outlet. It is a form of non-profit, cashless alternative economy which works at the grassroots level: a DIY economic system.

LETS first appeared in the 19th century and expanded in the 1930s during the great depression. They re-emerged in the 1970s – in response to high unemployment – when they were developed and redesigned to something like the present model.

"I hurt my back and had to lie flat for six long, depressing months," says Clare, a nurse and member of Beckford Community LETS. "On sick pay I couldn't afford pain-relieving treatment or help, so in desperation I joined LETS. Dozens of lovely people on LETS speeded my recovery with home help, Alexander technique, acupuncture and massage. I've repaid the scheme simply by baby-sitting, doing a bit of office work and selling a few things I didn't want."

The mention of Alexander technique, acupuncture and massage may raise the hackles of some who see LETS as

The LETS initiator
Liz Shephard, 43, lives in Warminster and has helped set up Local Exchange Trading Systems, or LETS, all over Britain and Europe. She got into LETS through her long-term involvement in the green movement which led her to realise that unless you change the way you measure economic performance you can't make much progress with issues like energy conservation and saving natural habitats.

She started work for the sustainable development group, the New Economics Foundation, when it was launched in 1984, researching community self-help schemes round the world. She explored their successes and failures and, keen to do something practical, helped draw up the NEF formula for setting up LETS in the UK.

In 1990 she started one of Britain's first LETS with the Warminster Friends of the Earth group. A key factor was the information packs they produced giving practical advice on how to set up a LETS.

"It takes a lot of commitment and hard work. When we began we had no funding and we worked a long run of 18-hour days. It's good to see how the idea that there are other ways to create wealth – and other means of measuring and valuing it – is beginning to spread."

a middle-class, hippy phenomenon designed to help the comfortably off swap small pleasures. This may have been true for some early schemes but LETS has come a long way since then, expanding in size and reaching a wide range of society.

In one example, a single mother of two was able to renovate her home without forking out cash. In return she baked and gardened for others. Other LETS schemes may involve lawn mower hire, car repairs, cleaning, graphic design, plumbing, music lessons, word processing, wine-making, video recording, baby sitting, accountancy and much more.

LETS is not necessarily about a direct exchange of services. Its strength is that it provides a structure for allowing a flow of work around a community. A member can earn "currency" from other members by helping them and he or she can then spend this whenever they like with anyone else on the scheme. The currency is in the form of barter tokens: Newberries, Beaks, Links, Cockles, Brights, Thanks, Acorns, Currents, Kreds and Olivers are all local versions of LETS currency around Britain.

There are five basic steps to setting up and running a LETS scheme:

1 Each member gets a Directory, a Chequebook and their own LETS account, starting at zero.
2 Everyone writes a list of their wants and offers to go in the directory.
3 They price their offers in the currency being used by their LETS, choosing their own value, or taking the going rate from the directory.
4 Members look in the directory for a service or goods they want and call the person offering it, fixing a time and agreeing a price if necessary.
5 The recipient pays by LETS cheque for the agreed amount once the job is done. The cheque is sent to the LETS accountant who credits the payee's account and debits the recipient's.

"At the end of the day no real money has been spent but every - body is better off," explains Nick, a member of Leicester LETS.

Like credit unions, LETS can help iron out cash flow problems, which can be particularly acute for those on low incomes. As LETS is an interest-free economy, you can start "spending" as

soon as you join, even if you haven't "earned" any currency. There are no credit or debit limits. To deter freeloading, the balance and turnover of all accounts are available to members so they can keep an eye on things.

Liz Shephard of LETS UK reckons the phenomenon could expand further but needs a central agency to promote it and help people to set schemes up. In the meantime, many local authorities are playing a supportive role: 25 per cent of LETS groups have some council help, generally under Local Agenda 21 – a 1992 Rio Earth Summit initiative which committed governments to promoting sustainable development through empowering communities, protecting the environment and sharing wealth, resources, opportunities and responsibilities. The support is usually "in kind" – for example providing meeting rooms or photocopying and printing facilities – although a few local authorities, including Calderdale and Frome district councils, actually trade in LETS. Several councils employ people to develop the schemes.

LETS are catching on internationally, with more than 300 schemes on the Continent, mainly in Holland, Germany, Italy and France, and the number is growing rapidly. LETS are big in Australia and New Zealand where the unemployed are often encouraged to join when they go to the dole office. In the United States there are about 150 Time Dollar schemes involving 10,000 members in deprived districts that exist mainly on welfare. The schemes, which cover services like education and care for the elderly and young children, are supported by local government and are tax-free.

The tax question is important. At the moment the Department of Social Security and the Inland Revenue accept that LETS should not be taxed because they cover welfare services and/or the income is below the tax threshold. However, some politicians and observers already regard LETS as a tax fiddle, so if some members were particularly successful in amassing credits these may end up being taxable or deducted from benefits.

Liz Shephard reckons tax thresholds should be high because LETS is a complementary system, not an income substitute. "It should be seen as a social currency, not as something that replaces the pound," she says. "Few people could live off LETS alone."

**World Development Movement
London 1987**

Photo: David Hoffman

STOP LLOYDS BANK
MAKING PROFITS OUT OF POVERTY

Left: A teach-in on
blacksmithing in Woking
Photo: Mark Beltran

Centre: The ethical clothing
chain store in Bradford on
Avon, which accepts 25 per
cent of payment in LETS

Right: Frome Wholefood Shop
which trades partly in LETS

~ FROME ~
WHOLEFOODS

TAYLORS
COFFEE
FRESHLY GROUND

A key advantage of LETS and other co-operative schemes is that they keep the benefits of trading within the local community. On their own, or combined with cash from other sources such as Government grants, subsidies or welfare payments, they can contribute to reviving financially depressed areas, says Ruth Hobson of the New Economics Foundation. "LETS systems are interest free, so they can't be siphoned out of local communities to invest more profitably in Hong Kong or Taiwan," she explains. "They can't be used to play the money markets or the roulette tables because they only exist as relationships between members."

Every community has tremendous human resources, but often there are no systems or structures to encourage people to use them to improve their living standards. Worst of all, attacks on the current benefits system, like the Job Seekers Allowance, actually dissuade people from working voluntarily, despite the opportunity to improve the quality of life.

For those with money to spend, save and invest, there are the relatively new developments of ethical investment and fair trade. These work on a more global scale than LETS, community banking or co-operatives, but they are based on the same philosophy: customers pay a fair price for decent goods and services that are produced, often co-operatively, with due regard to the workers and environment.

"Fair trade is a good example of community economic action, in that it directly links communities right across the world," says Ed Mayo, of the New Economics Foundation. "Relationships are created, short circuiting the global economy, and building real responsibilities, ethics and values."

So, the theory is in place, the practices are growing and the ideas are catching on but this does not necessarily guarantee that setting up a community economic scheme will always produce financial gains and increased self reliance. Many of the schemes have a precarious existence: food co-ops can be forced out of business if there is competition from discount warehouses; the hard work involved means organisers can simply run out of steam; and unrelated community problems can prevent schemes from taking firm root.

"Credit unions can make people feel more secure," says Jim Dearlove of the Birmingham Credit Union Development Agency. "They are not going to change the world or act as a panacea for everything, but they have their part in a broader movement."

Ironically, although community economic schemes can make the greatest impact on low income communities, they are developing more slowly in those areas. This may be caused by low self-confidence and the general pressures of daily survival which leave little time and energy for trying something new and alternative. However, there is potential, says Liz Shephard, "providing these self-help schemes are not regarded by the Government as an excuse to cut benefits."

"One of the assumptions of economic theory is that people are self interested, that altruism is irrational economically," says Ed Mayo. "People become the kind of people that economics assumes they are: individualistic, concerned with commodities and accumulation, with their role as consumers not citizens, selfish. So it starts off with a set of ridiculous assumptions about the environment and people, and it ends up by shaping society in that form, which is why economics is really politics by the back door.

"If you can change people's view of economics to make them believe it is something that is relevant to their community and that they can control, then you are making progress towards real political change."

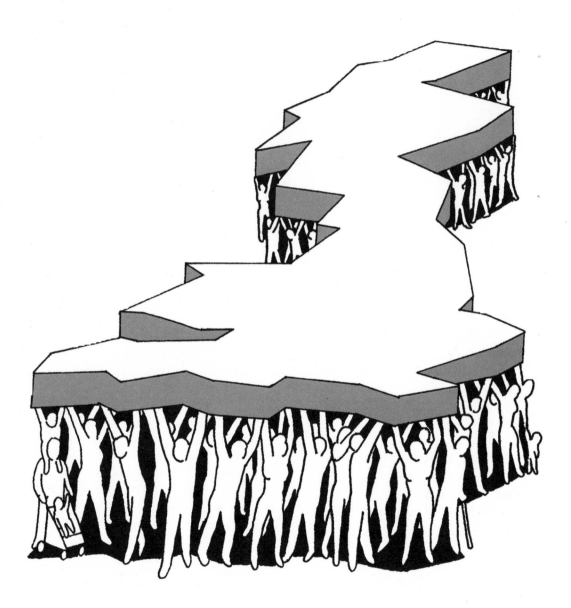

Illustration: Paul Render

The Future

"We are the new people, we are the old people

We are the same people, stronger than before"

Campfire chant sung by DIYers and Liverpool dockers on a joint march and rally in September 1996

So far so good, but what now? How do DIY activists turn radical protest against a system that doesn't listen or seem to care into a positive agenda for sustainable political, economic and social change? Can they create a different and widely-accepted set of priorities and new ways of making and implementing policies? In other words, can DIY Culture have lasting relevance to society as a whole?

The short answer is yes… probably. While this book was being written, DIY Culture has been evolving, embracing wider concerns and involving people who might have felt alienated by alternative politics and lifestyles. The movement has proved it is not some short-term fad for people with nothing better to do, but that it is putting down deep roots among a wide range of people whose lives have been changed deeply by the empowering experience of radical protest or by opting out of mainstream society.

Even those in power have begun to listen. The former Conservative Transport Minister Steven Norris admitted, in March 1997 while the Tories were still in power, that much of the Conservative Government's road-building plans in the 1980s and early 1990s were misguided. He said that the wrong route had been chosen for the Newbury bypass which was the scene of some of the most dramatic anti -roads action and heavy-handed policing.

In the same week, the Department of Transport put on hold plans for a bypass for Salisbury after environmentalists made a strong case that it would destroy water meadows that are home to a variety of bird species. The Department said all sides should get together to discuss the best options for solving traffic congestion in the area, including localised road widening – and all this without a single treehouse being built or an inch of protest tunnel being excavated. At the time of writing, we don't know the outcome of these consultations or whether they are just a cosmetic exercise to throw environmentalists off the scent. But they are a start.

The challenge now is to build on this kind of recognition and open channels of communication to the new Labour Government so that those who hold political, economic and social power will listen to those who have justified grievances. People who are radical, committed and uncompromising should be respected for what they say and stand for, and should have a part in shaping the future. DIYers need to spread their influence and support so that they are no longer just a visible, minority irritant to the authorities. They must show that they represent a wide cross section of society.

"If you had a mobilised and active public who really were determined to stop things happening, the Government couldn't bully through laws and decisions," says Sarah Wise, Direct Communications Campaigner at Greenpeace.

Lyndsay Cooke, Marketing and Communications Officer for the constitutional reform pressure group Charter 88, reckons this process of mobilisation has already begun. "People are beginning to discover things that they share that matter to them," she explains. "It is an immense surprise and hugely positive in terms of the future that those values are held in common by the middle-class, middle-aged voter who is outraged by animal exports in Brightlingsea and by the traveller who wants the right to go to a free festival."

One example of a potential way forward is the links that have been forged between DIYers and parts of the traditional labour movement. Reclaim the Streets held street protests in the summer of 1996 to support the RMT rail union in their dispute with London Underground over staffing; greens joined miners and local communities in their campaign against open-cast mining; National Union of Mineworkers leader Arthur Scargill, who heads the Socialist Labour Party (which has a radical environmental policy), addressed an open meeting against the Newbury bypass.

Above: **Summer 1996**
The Reclaim the Streets banner
amoung many other supporters on
a rally through Liverpool City centre

Photo: Nick Cobbing

Opposite: **Protester and Dockers
wife Liverpool, September 1996**
The initial scepticism became
replaced with friendship as the two
cultures got to know one another

Photo: Nick Cobbing

Then, Reclaim the Streets, the Green Party, EcoTrip, the
Freedom Network and other DIY groups joined in support
for the 500 Liverpool dockers who were sacked by the
Mersey Docks and Harbour Company for going on strike
after one worker was dismissed for refusing to work overtime
when his wife was in labour. Labour relations at the port
had been strained because the dockers had been attempting
to block imports of toxic waste.

THE ATMOSPHERE ON THE MARCH WAS GOOD AND THERE WAS A REAL MIXTURE OF GROUPS.

The DIYers helped organise a 10,000-strong march and rally in Liverpool in September 1996, to mark the first year of the strike, and an even bigger demonstration in London in April 1997. Both events were a slightly strange combination of traditional labour movement commitment and DIY innovation: brass bands and bagpipes competed with techno music; trade union banners mingled with anarchist flags; and families in official strikers' T shirts chatted with multi-coloured, dreadlocked cyclists.

The joint activities entailed a learning curve for everyone involved. "We were working with the dockers for six or seven weeks before the September march," says Sam of Reclaim the Streets. "There was a lot of distrust at the beginning as each side didn't know where the other was coming from. We were worried that the dockers might be very hard left with fixed ideas and they were worried that we were young, crusty anarchists."

Bobby Morton, one of the dockers' leaders, describes the alliance as: "A historic meeting. Old-time industrialists who were ultra-organised meeting what seemed like a bunch of people who frowned on organisation."

However, both sides soon came to appreciate each other's strengths. "The dockers were quite paternal really and were looking out for us," says Sam about the September demonstration. "The atmosphere on the march was good and there was a real mixture of groups. It was much less dire than the standard marches and that is what the dockers wanted."

Morton agrees: "The DIY people brought their exuberance and gave us a tremendous boost. Both marches were a great success."

At the September event, EcoTrip had occupied a vacant Customs and Excise building for the Saturday night to provide accommodation, food and a party for people who had travelled

from outside Liverpool. Dockers, their families and supporters put people up and one local pub provided crash space with free food and beer thrown in. Sunday, the day after the march, was workshops, briefings and a chance for dockers and DIYers to talk politics. The weekend ended with speeches of thanks and, of course, word-perfect singing of Beatles songs.

"The dockers are not 'greenies', their perspective is centralist left," says Green Party activist Shane Collins, who helped organise the events. "Due to lack of support from the trade union leadership and the Labour Party, they have formed incredibly strong ties in their local community – in a way that most greens just dream about – and on an international level with dockers around the world.

"However, we are both against the same things – such as global capitalism and imports of toxic waste – and through more contact between us the dockers will see the inherent connections between social justice and environmental

Manchester Airport Protest
April 1997
Swampy, a veteran of anti-roads
action at Newbury and Fairmile,
at the entrance to his tunnel

Photo: Andrew Testa

protection and the greens will get an understanding of the sort of tight-knit self-supporting communities we want to build. This is the basis for firm and welcome alliances."

These alliances are already beginning to happen. As this book was going to press, a dockers delegation was on its way to support protesters against the second runway proposed for Manchester Airport. "We discovered that we share a concern for the future," says Morton. "We're trying to make sure that the youth of Merseyside have a good future in terms of a decent environment and secure jobs. Reclaim the Streets' ideas revolve around the future of the planet and of local communities."

The important thing for all sides now is to begin emphasising these joint aims. The time has come for DIY activists to stop just saying "No" to someone else's agenda and to start building a vision of how they want society to be. The problem is that there is a huge leap from using inventive stunts to expose what's wrong with the system, to agreeing how it should be put right, and by who.

The proponents of DIY Culture are only too aware of the uphill task ahead. "I don't expect to see change but I do want to see the beginning of something," says Peter Hope of the disabled people's Direct Action Network. "That is all that I can actually aspire to."

Even this entails coming up with real positive alternatives. "It is very important to start learning the arguments, the enemies, the territory, the facts," says Emma Must, one of the co-ordinators of the anti-roads group Alarm UK. "We need to be able to put our answers forward, not just whinging and stamping our feet all the time. We must discover other solutions."

These sentiments are seconded by George Monbiot, a researcher at Green College, Oxford and founder of the land rights group, The Land is Ours. "We must stop responding

West Wood site, Lyminge Forest Protest May 1997
Rattrap camp protester Blue prepares his tunnel to challenge Rank Organization's plans to build a pleasure park on the site of ancient Lyminge Forest.

Photo: Tim Hetherington

to Government policy, we must start creating our own policies and forcing the Government to respond to us, because political change of any real and lasting value can only happen if we are setting the agenda rather than responding to someone else's."

Monbiot points out that there is already a system and structures in place that can be used for this purpose, so why reinvent the wheel? There is great potential to use existing environmental law at a practical level, for example, to prevent contractors using heavy machinery near badger sets that are in use, explains long-time green and peace campaigner Rowan Tilly, who is now active in the anti-arms trade Ploughshares network.

"It is important to use this notion of upholding the law," she says. "Campaigners against whaling and other issues of the seas have used international law and agreements for years as a defence for their actions. I hope more people take up this theme. There is lots of scope, for instance with factories

that are breaking pollution laws. Taking the law into your own hands is an excellent example of participatory democracy."

George Monbiot wants to go still further, to use the mainstream political process to support the wider concerns of DIY Culture. "We can save ourselves an awful lot of headaches if we can get our concerns onto the Government's agenda," he points out.

However, some commentators, such as John Vidal, Environment Editor of The Guardian, warn DIY activists to hold onto their ideals and not get absorbed into the mainstream. "A death of a lot of interesting social movements is when politicians start taking a close interest," he claims.

Others dismiss this concern. "There is absolutely no point in having two systems co-existing which don't talk to each other," says Geoff Mulgan, Director of the centre-left think-tank Demos. "The reality is that although there are lots of ways

GOOD FRIDAY, APRIL 1997, AT THE NO RUNWAY 2 CAMP IN CHESHIRE

Agnes Galway, DIY activist

"I slept in one of the communal benders – well, more just lay there. Perhaps it had something to do with being up a tree, in a howling gale, with a thin sleeping bag, underneath a flight path which was taking the brunt of the bank holiday getaways.

The treehouse was in the Sir Cliff Richard camp (named after the cliff it sits under), where all the vegans and gentler hippies hung out, as opposed to Babylon camp where the meat eaters lived and where we sang, drank and revelled all night. Each of the camps has its own identity: River Rats, mainly women by the river; Zion tree camp; Wild Garlic, furthest away in lovely woodland, less muddy and tidier. They are all linked by CB radio.

It's a mixture of primitive camping and high technology: mud, mobile phones, camcorders with lights powered by a car battery. Even one guy with a personal organiser and Justin in his Barber jacket (turns out he was the barman in the local near the Fairmile camp in Devon and joined the protest). There were accents from everywhere. We were south of Manchester but you

wouldn't have guessed – lilts of the West Country, mixed with a bit of London, Nottingham and Derby, with the odd Frenchman and one unnerving loud American drawl.

In the morning everyone sat around the fire warming up, talking about the night's "pixying" success. The whole site has recently been surrounded by a seven foot wire fence but it is proving difficult to keep it whole, as mysteriously each night, large holes appear where the wire has been neatly clipped away. Posts are strangely bent or pulled out completely and the barbed wire that used to run along the top is strewn along the ground. And right under the noses of the security men – must be the pixies.

We were still waking and warming up by the fire when the Parish Councillor came by. He is also the village baker and had brought 80 fresh hot-cross buns. He wasn't the only local that day at Babylon, there was a steady line of visitors shyly bearing plastic bags full of food.

Each camp has a communal covered area with a fire, logs and

crates for people to sit on and a kitchen tent/bender with all the stores in it. The kettle is on a hook over the fire, or just balanced on the burning sticks. There's a washing up area with bowl and water, next to the kitchen. All connected with pallets lying sunken in the mud, meant to act as a walkway with a grip, but more a slippery shute. Recycling bins – aluminium cans, bottles, paper, tin cans – all full and organised, nothing out of place.

Between the camps, steps are cut into steep hills, the odd "No Runway 2" board is fastened on the perimeter fence where yellow-jacketed security guards shift their weight from foot to foot. A few policemen lurk at the top of the hill filming protestors filming them – both sides finding the humour in the situation.

The eviction is just weeks away, there is work to be done and people are building. Up trees, on platforms, in harnesses, nailing planks together and building frames. Communal treehouses are made in low places, better for those unused to climbing with mud on their boots in the dark up an unfamiliar tree. Others are

high up in the top branches of tall trees, their dark shapes like giant crows' nests waving in the wind. These are attached to each other and other trees by walkways. That is where the cat-and-mouse evictions using climbers will happen. Meanwhile, down below, a warren of tunnels is taking shape.

As the day wears on people head home dirty and tired. A girl tries to learn to balance on the rope walkway – without much luck. A guy demonstrates how to do it but makes it look more difficult with arms and legs at crazy angles. A big tea-drinking session gets underway in a large, cosy bender with lots of discussion about climbing harnesses. A group of "tourists" being shown round the camp peer in nervously.

Then it's dinner, more drinking and singing of rebel songs and poetry raps… and sleep. This time, as more people gradually crept into the communal treehouse, I joined the line of sleeping-bagged bodies. One of the first lessons of camp life is that sharing body heat is the only way to last the night."

in which the new politics does impact and reverberate on people's daily lives, there are still loads of other issues which are determined by what politicians decide in Parliament. It is completely naive to think that is not the case."

Des Kaye, co-founder and co-ordinator of Kingston Green Fair, tries to think of the future as a partnership. "Instead of looking at an enemy, we need to find areas of similarity where we can work together," he says. "This requires a change in attitude from all areas. That has to be the way forward, instead of this Socialist Workers Party mentality of destroy the state and then build up. We have a system, we have an establishment and we can utilise them."

This partnership needs effective communication: a clear political language, free of rhetoric, that really answers ordinary people's questions and embraces healthy debate. Andrew Marr, Editor of The Independent, thinks it is possible "if politicians discover some of their old roles – as people who lead opinion because we trust them and are interested in them. Who don't feel they have to control everything."

The other side of this is that DIYers need to participate in the mainstream to change that which they complain about – even voting and being elected, reversing the trend over the last decade of fewer young people bothering to vote. And it doesn't stop there, particularly for those DIYers who take the view that the whole system is diseased and not designed to give the public a voice but to concentrate political and economic power in the hands of a few. Everyone needs to take more interest in their surroundings and community: if the future is about a process of improvement, people need to look their own obligations.

"We need a stronger public," says Helen Wilkinson, Project Director of Demos. "It is easy to blame the system and the politicians but you need to ask people to make choices and take responsibility. We need a huge self-education process if the ethos of the new politics is to be sustainable because there is a bit in people which still wants somebody up there to blame when things go wrong."

However, greater democracy and grassroots involvement has its price. Decision-making would be slower and often less clear-cut. "The more local communities and DIY politics are

empowered, the harder it is to have effective national strategies for some things," says Andrew Marr. "But in the end that is a price worth paying to give people more of a sense of ownership and control over their lives and neighbourhoods."

A framework already exists to assist that process: Agenda 21 – a 500-page document endorsed by more than 150 nations at the 1992 United Nations Environment Summit in Rio de Janeiro. It sets out why countries should work towards sustainable development and how they can do so. It is a tool that can help people take care of their own communities: but only if they want to take that responsibility.

"Agenda 21 is the best thing that has ever happened," says Des Kaye. "It is a blueprint for sustainability, for co-operation and agreement, for drawing in the local community. Potentially there is a lot of hope."

Quietly, up and down the country, many thousands of people have been using Agenda 21 to carry out consultation exercises to discover what people like and dislike about their neighbourhoods. Local authorities have a central role, often in partnership with environmental or community groups. Julian Agyeman, founder and former Chair of the Black Environment Network, has been drawing up a report on ethnic minorities and sustainable development for the Local Government Management Board. He emphasises that the issue has much wider social and economic implications than many people realise.

"Sustainable development is not just about green concerns. It is about building a stable, safe and secure community where groups such as ethnic minorities and elderly people can go out without fear of attack," he explains. "There are narrow and broad definitions of 'environment'. Lots of groups are protecting their local environment through anti-racist work, equality initiatives and inner-city regeneration. The links with sustainable development need to be recognised and strengthened."

However, very little is going to happen tomorrow because the wheels of change in national (and some local) institutions move very slowly. And there is stubborn resistance from some of those in power who do not want to hand over control to the grassroots. Meanwhile, the process of empowerment is being undermined by the security forces who are against any weakening of the state and have therefore been bugging and burgling the homes of animal rights protesters and other DIY activists.

"People shouldn't underestimate the ability of the state to repress things like this," says Steve-Platt, journalist and former Editor of New Statesman and Society. "I am waiting for the first conspiracy charges to be laid against anti-roads protesters. So far the state and the police have been relatively easy-going, they have not used the full force of their power to come down on people."

Stopping the flow of money to those involved in DIY Culture through reducing benefits is another way to stop it growing. "Even though people like myself probably work harder than people who have jobs, my work has no monetary value so the state will do whatever they can to stop me doing it," complains Adrian of the Dragon Environmental Network. "They can force me to take a job that pays £3 an hour and makes someone else rich. The ways they can do this, through measures like the Job Seekers Allowance, are getting stronger."

Despite the efforts of DIYers and others fighting for a fairer society, the gulf is growing between rich and poor, and between those in power and those who feel so alienated by the system that they can't see the point of voting in elections. Geoff Mulgan of Demos thinks this is dangerous: "It can lead to a vicious circle because if people are not connected, the Government doesn't feel any pressure to provide them with help to get jobs and homes. They in turn think that the Government isn't doing anything for them, so why should they get involved? You end up with a miserable, divided society where one group is almost parasitically keeping hold of the power. You could imagine Britain going somewhere down that route."

Some DIY activists believe we're already there. "In our generation there is a vein of hopelessness and nihilism," says one. "We are in a car heading towards a cliff, the accelerator is down and there is nothing we can do about it so we may as well have a good time. All care for humanity goes out the window. That is why there is a resurgence in the use of heroin."

As this book was being edited, Britain had a new Government. Few DIYers, or long-time activists in the labour movement or alternative politics, held out any great hopes of radical change. All the mainstream parties exist to manage capitalism, not to overthrow it. However, a new Government brings opportunities and even optimism: different leaders, with different approaches and priorities. History is full of political swings and surprises, so something could happen here. It is up to those involved in DIY Culture to keep up the pressure.

"Protest offers a different vision that can inspire people with a set of ideals and politics," says Heritage Secretary Chris Smith. "Politics is effectively about making the compromises that will always be necessary between the ideal and the real. Unless you have people on the outside of the system constantly saying 'this is the ideal that we think ought to be achieved', the whole process is going to be diminished."

But can this pressure really influence what's going on in the corridors of power? "It's hard to predict," says Adrian. "I've seen things happen which I would never have dreamt of. If somebody had said to me that I would be stopping the traffic in Greenwich High Street and local people would have been coming up and patting me on the back, I would have said, 'Come on, no way'."

John Bird, Editor-in-Chief of The Big Issue, thinks DIY Culture will continue to grow as people increasingly feel able to take decisions about their own lives. "I never believed all that crap about 'Thatcher's Children'," he says. "The idea that people go through a process like 18 years of Conservative Government and come out greedy, selfish, small minded and individualistic is not backed up by the people I've seen within DIY Culture."

Sam of Reclaim the Streets sees the movement fitting into a broader resurgence of radical politics. "We're anti-capitalism and we're interested in the wider struggles," she says. "We're not utopians or visionaries: a vision of the future is a naive thing to have. The ethic of socialism that grew up over the last century is dying. Now DIY is working again to restore it without using the old words which frighten people."

A who's who of DIY Media

- **The Freedom Network (FN)** acts as a focal point for anyone needing information within the DIY scene. It started as an alliance of different groups that opposed or were going to be directly affected by the Criminal Justice and Public Order Act 1994 (CJA) – including travellers, squatters and hunt sabs – who wanted to highlight the dangers of the proposed legislation. They were originally based in the squatted Cooltan arts and community centre in south London but moved on when everyone was evicted.

  There are now about 120 local networks across Britain acting as a contact point for the media, other groups and the public. Since the CJA became law, many FN activists have channelled their experience into other issues but a core of people still exists, geared towards looking for practical ways to protect and develop sustainable, alternative lifestyles.

- **The Free Information Network (FIN)** consists of a loose and changing alliance of about 15 regional newsheets with a central philosophy of providing a free, participatory self-creating media. It grew out of the free festival movement in the mid-1980s, publicising details of festivals, gigs, demos and actions, confronting issues that were ignored or misrepresented by the mainstream media. The groups vary from relatively large well-organised organisations to smaller ones such as CreweFin which is basically one guy who was made redundant from British Rail and decided to set up his own information campaign. His actions include leafletting Crewe station when a nuclear convoy comes through to alert locals to the danger.

- **Squall** is a quarterly magazine which reports on all forms of DIY Culture. It has a print run of 8,000 – although the readership is far higher – and tries to reach a diverse audience, including doctors, lawyers, teachers, occupational therapists, travellers, squatters and full-time campaigners. The aim is to reduce the suspicion and intolerance between people with different interests and lifestyles. The magazine was set up following the statement in 1992 by Kenneth Baker, who was then Home Secretary, that the Government was going to "get tough on armed robbers, tough on rapists and tough on squatters". This farcical juxtaposition received no media comment at all. So a team of committed people launched a magazine to counter the hysterical political tirade being heaped on squatters.

  Squall's approach is to be well presented, accurate and investigative, and in a very short time they have uncovered many stories of national significance. Members of the collective subsequently ended up appearing on countless television and radio programmes as spokespersons for and on squatters, travellers, youth issues, criminality, drugs, protest, graffiti, the campaign to support Dave Morris and Helen Steel – the environmental activists being sued by McDonald's – and a multitude of other street issues.

- **SchNEWS** is produced by Brighton Justice? one of the most active DIY groups in the country. SchNEWS has become one of the most informative and important underground newsheets. Three thousand are printed weekly, but it is estimated that the readership could be up to 20,000 through copying and the SchNEWS Internet site. SchNEWS provides weekly snapshots of positive direct action including: protests against the Criminal Justice Act; pickets to stop trucks carrying live animal exports; and actions against French nuclear tests in the South Pacific.

- **Undercurrents** is a series of alternative news videos which show protests and other issues from the point of view of those involved. Undercurrents began in April 1994 and has built an estimated audience of 100,000, not just among hard-core activists: the videos are available in libraries, schools and colleges and shown at public meetings.

- **Conscious Cinema** is a Brighton-based collective making videos along the same lines as Undercurrents, though more regularly and in a more immediate and uncut form. Copies of the videos go to clubs, pubs, meetings and conferences in Britain and 15 other countries. The videos can be obtained free providing they are returned so that the next edition can be recorded over the top. In 1996 Conscious Cinema combined with a live reading of SchNEWS to create Schlive, a constantly - evolving, travelling media show that aims to demonstrate the effects of the Criminal Justice Act and other related issues.

- **Phreak** is a web site designed to provide a platform on the Internet for people to communicate and exchange views and news. Although real-time conferencing is in its infancy on the Net, Phreak hopes to implement this in future to allow users to discuss issues directly.

- **Urban75** is a new web site which is a central resource for rave culture, protests and explaining the law and effects of drugs. It has a huge activists' database as well as providing an outlet for its new interactive game featuring "Slap a politician" and "Slap a Spice Girl".

  See Appendix two for addresses and contacts.

Appendix one:
The Essence of DIY Culture

1. DIY Culture draws on a long tradition of grassroots movements that has existed over the centuries in many different forms.

2. People involved have usually been personally affected by the activities of the authorities or big business.

3. DIY Culture involves a shift from apathy to action, a realisation that it is no good sitting around complaining about things.

4. Many people doing it have no faith in conventional politics as a means of change.

5. It is born out of a sense of frustration with tried and tested methods of protest; people start trying a different approach because the old one doesn't work.

6. DIY Culture is about people formulating their own lifestyles, creating their own systems, setting their own agendas, raising their own issues, using their own vocabulary and finding their own ways to deal with problems rather than waiting for someone else to do it.

7. People are living these systems and agendas, not just talking about them.

8. DIY Culture has no unifying politics or ideology. It tends to be individualistic.

9. A diverse range of people is involved.

10. The Criminal Justice and Public Order Act 1994 acted as a strong focus for DIY Culture, bringing many of the diverse groups into contact with each other.

11. DIY Culture is associated with a revival of non-violent direct action: protests against the M3 extension through Twyford Down in Hampshire were a catalyst.

12. The people involved in DIY Culture often feel empowered by the experience.

13. Some DIY Culture is linked with the mainstream media, using innovative direct action to capture the attention of national newspapers, television and radio, thereby raising issues and stimulating debate.

14. DIY Culture also has its own media to carry news and information that the mainstream media ignore, to keep in contact and address important issues.

A more complete listing can be found in SchNewsRound which contains the definitive Yellow Pages of DIY groups in the UK. Orders to Justice? (c/o On the Fiddle, PO Box 2600, Brighton, East Sussex). Price £4.99 including p&p.

Advance Party Network
Information and actions for party-goers and organisers
PO Box 3290, London NW2 3UJ
T: 0181 450 6929
e-mail: fimone@sypte.co.uk

Advisory Service for Squatters
Offers legal and practical advice on squatting
2 St Pauls Road, London, N1 2QN
T: 0171 359 8814 F: 0171 359 5185

Alarm UK
National networking group for anti-roads community campaigns
9-10 College Terrace, London E3 5AN
T/F: 0181 983 3572

Animal Aid
Campaigns against all animal cruelty
The Old Chapel, Bradford Street, Tonbridge, Kent TN9 1AW
T: 01732 364546 F: 01732 366533
Spice of Life veggie hotline: 01732 354032

Antil-Racist Alliance
Black-led organisation that aims to tackle racism
PO Box 2578, London N5 1UF
T: 0171 278 6869

Big Issue
Britain's largest selling current affairs magazine with centres throughout the UK. The magazine is unique in that it is sold on the streets by homeless and ex-homeless people.
Fleet House, 57-61 Clerkenwell Road, London EC1M 5NP
T: 0171 418 0418 F: 0171 418 0428
e-mail: london@bigissue.co.uk

Birmingham Credit Union Development Agency
Supports the setting up and running of credit unions
2nd Floor, City Gate House, 25 Moat Lane, Birmingham B56 BH
T: 0121 622 1062 F: 0121 622 7042

Black Environment Network
Networking organisation creating opportunities for ethnic communities to participate in environmental matters
9 Llainwen Uchaf, Llanberis, Gwynedd, Wales LL55 4LL
T/F: 01286 870715

Camcorder Action Network
Films direct actions and is creating an archive for the future
c/o Undercurrents, 16B Cherwell Street, Oxford OX4 1BG
T: 01865 203663

Campaign Against the Asylum and Immigration Bill
c/o ACAPA, St Hildas East Community Centre, 18 Club Row, London E2 7EY

Campaign Against the Arms Trade (CAAT)
Campaigns for an end to all arms trading beginning with British exports. Organises events and actions, publishes research
11 Goodwin Street, London N4 3HQ
T: 0171 281 0297 F: 0171 281 4369
e-mail: caat@gn.apc.org
website: http://www.gn.apc.org/caat

Centre for Alternative Technology
Working model for a community based on sustainable, alternative technology
Machynlleth, Powys, Wales SY20 9AZ
T: 01654 702400 F: 01654 702782
e-mail: cat@gn.apc.org
website: http://www.foe.co.uk/cat

Centre for the Study of Environmental Change (CSEC)
Research and publications
Bowland Tower East, Lancaster University, Lancaster LA1 4YF
T: 01524 592658 F: 01524 846339
e-mail: csec@lancaster.ac.uk

CHAR
Housing campaign for single people, runs the GROUNDSWELL project which promotes self-help projects
5-15 Cromer St, London WC1H 8LS
T: 0171 833 2071 F: 0171 278 6685

Charter 88
Campaigns for greater democracy, particularly the reform of Britain's electoral system and for more open and accessible government
Exmouth House, 3-11 Pine Street, London EC1R OJH
T: 0171 833 1988 F: 0171 833 5895
e-mail: admin@charter88.org.uk

Communities Against Toxics
Collects information on hazardous waste and supports communities fighting polluting developments in their neighbourhoods
PO Box 29, Ellesmere Port, South Wirral, L66 3TX
T: 0151 339 5473 F: 0151 201 6780
e-mail: cats@gn.apc.org

Compassion in World Farming
Lobby group for humane farming practices
c/o Eve Hodson, 23 Dulverton Mansions, Grays Inn Road, London WC1
T: 0171 837 0284

Conscious Cinema
Monthly video round-up of protests and related social justice campaigns
PO Box 2679, Brighton, East Sussex BN2 IUJ
e-mail: cinema@phreak.intermedia.co.uk

Conviction
Campaigns for and supports prisoners falsely accused or imprisoned
PO Box 522, Sheffield S1 3FF

Critical Mass
National direct action campaign for a safe bicycle network. Central London Critical Mass is at 6pm on the last Friday of every month, underneath the southern end of Waterloo Bridge
Contact: Patrick Field T: 0171 249 3779
e-mail: patrick@neuronet.co.uk

DEMOS
Independent think-tank committed to creating radical perspectives on the long-term problems facing the UK and other advanced industrial societies
9 Bridewell Place, London EC4V 6AP
T: 0171 353 4479 F: 0171 353 4481
e-mail: demos@demon.co.uk

Disabled Peoples Direct Action Network
Support and action network campaigning for civil rights, with a focus on transport issues
3 Crawley Road, London N22 6AN
T: 0181 889 1361

Dongas Tribe
Peaceful anti-roads campaigners
c/o Chris, 6 East Street, West Coker, Yeovil, Somerset

Dragon Environmental Network
Non-violent direct action pagan environmentalists
3 Sandford Walk, London SE14 6NB
T: 0181 691 7685

Earth First!
Nationwide network of autonomous direct action environmental groups
PO Box 9656, London N4 4JY
T: 0171 561 9146

English Collective of Prostitutes
Campaigns for the rights of workers in the sex industry
PO Box 287, London NW6 5QU

Exodus Collective
Free party and housing collective in Luton
Long Meadow Community Farm, Chalton Cross, Sundown Road, Luton, Beds
T: 01582 508936
e-mail: 101370.336@compuserve.com.uk

Faslane Peace Camp
Permanent camp outside the Clyde Trident nuclear submarine base
Shandon, Helensburgh, Dunbartonshire, Scotland
T: 01436 820901

Festival Eye
Magazine on festivals, protests and travellers
BCM Box 2002, London WC1N 3XX

Football Fans Against the CJA
Provides information and assists football fans targetted by the Criminal Justice and Public Order Act 1994
352 Southwyck House, Moorlands Estate, London SW9 8TT
web site: http://www.display.co.uk/ffacja

Contacts

Freedom Network
Information on national and local DIY actions
and events
PO Box 9384, London SW9 7ZB
T: 0171 582 3474 **Action Line:** 0171 793 7343

Free Information Network
Produces newsheets with information on festivals,
parties, events, meetings and campaigns. To receive
material send SAE and donation to local branch
AberdeenFIN, 36 Buchan Road, Torry,
Aberdeen AB1 3SW
CamFIN, c/o Arjuna, 12 Mill Road,
Cambridge CB1 2AD
EFFIN, c/o York, The Coffee Bar Grassroots,
58 Charles Street, Cardiff
GuilFin, PO Box 217, Guildford, Surrey
MaidstonFIN, PO Box 263, Maidstone, Kent
MerseyFIN, PO Box 110, Liverpool L69 6AU
MotherClan, 29 Silverton Crescent, Moseley,
Birmingham B13 9NH
NeverNeverFIN, 8 Campbell Road, Southsea, Hants
NottFIN, c/o The Rainbow Centre,
180 Mansfield Road, Nottingham
Oxfiend, Box A, 111 Magdalen Road, Oxford
RatFINk, c/o RSI, 30 Silver Street, Reading
ShefFIN, The Ecology Co,
199 Crookes Valley Road, Sheffield
SouthWestFIN, c/o Wild Pear Court,
Combe Martin, North Devon
WalsallFIN, c/o 17 Newhall House, Newhall Street,
Cladmore, Walsall WS1 3DY
ChildrensFIN, c/o Brambles Housing Co-op,
82 Andover Street, Sheffield S3 9EH

Friends, Families and Travellers Support Group
Advice and information for travellers
Top Floor, 33 High Street, Glastonbury,
Somerset BA6 9H7
T/F: 01458 832371

Friends of the Earth
Environmental campaigning organisation
26-28 Underwood Street, London N1 7JQ
T: 0171 490 1555
web site: http://www.foe.co.uk

Frontline
Magazine covering travellers, parties and protests
Victoria Road, Yarmouth, Isle of Wight PO41 OQW
T: 01983 760956

Greenhouse
Community environmental and resource centre for
activists and campaign groups
46-48 Bethel Street, Norwich, Norfolk NR2 1NR
T: 01603 631007 **F:** 01603 666879

Green Party
1A Waterlow Road, London N19 5NJ
T: 0171 272 4474 **F:** 0171 272 6653
e-mail: greenpartyuk@gn.apc.org

Greenpeace International
Environmental campaigning organisation
Canonbury Villas, London N1 2PN
T: 0171 865 8100
web site: http://www.greenpeace.org

Groundswell - see CHAR

Hunt Saboteurs Association
National umbrella organisation for local groups
PO Box 2786, Brighton, East Sussex BN2 2AX
T: 01273 622827
e-mail: hsa@gn.apc.org.uk

Institute of Race Relations
Educational charity researching into and publishing
information on racism and how to fight it
2-6 Leeke Street, London WC1 9HS
T: 0171 837 0041

Inquest
Provides information and support for the friends
and relatives of those who die at work, in custody
and where there are issues of public safety
Ground Floor, Alexandra House, 330 Seven Sisters
Road, London N4 2PJ
T: 0181 802 7450

Justice?
Activist networking group and producer of weekly
newsletter SchNEWS
c/o On the Fiddle, PO Box 2600,
Brighton, East Sussex
T: 01273 685913
e-mail: Justice@intermedia.co.uk

Kings Hill Collective
Low-impact rural community
Cock Mill Lane, East Pennard, Somerset BA4 6TR
T: 01749 860660

Kingston Green Fair
One of Britain's largest environmental events
8 Crescent Road, Kingston, Surrey KT2 7QR
T: 0181 546 1827

The Land is Ours
Campaigns for land for homes, livelihoods and life
Box E, 111 Magdalen Road, Oxford OX4 1RQ
T: 01865 722016
e-mail: tlio@gn.apc.org
website: http://www.envirolink.org/orgs/tlio/

League Against Cruel Sports
Campaigns against hunting, shooting
and blood sports
83-87 Union Street, London SE1 1SG
T: 0171 403 6155 **F:** 0171 403 4532

Legal Defence and Monitoring Group
Provides legal observers, advice, training
and support
BM Box HAVEN, London WC1X 3NN
T: 0181 802 9804

Lesbian Avengers
Direct action group committed to raising lesbian
visibility and rights
PO Box 501, London SE21 7DS
T: 0181 852 3956

Letslink UK
Network of Local Exchange Trading Systems
61 Woodstock Road, Warminster, Wiltshire BA12 9DH
T: 01985 217871

Liberty (National Council for Civil Liberties)
Lobbying organisation for civil liberties
21 Tabard Street, London SE1 4LA
T: 0171 403 3888

Liverpool Dockers Campaign
Supports and builds solidarity for the sacked dockers
and their families and raises environmental issues
c/o TGWU, Transport House, 37 Islington,
Liverpool L3 8EQ
T: 0151 207 3388 **F:** 0151 207 0696

Lloyds and Midland Boycott
Encourages students to boycott banks involved
in Third World debt
c/o Grassroots, Manchester University Students
Union, Oxford Road, Manchester M13 9PR
T: 0161 274 4665
e-mail: msex3jp1@stud.man.ac.uk

McLibel Support Campaign
Information on court case brought by McDonald's
against two green activists, plus support for the
defendants and news of further protests
c/o London Greenpeace, 5 Caledonian Road,
London N1 9DX
T/F: 0171 713 1269
web site: http://www.mcspotlight.org

New Economics Foundation
Promotes practical and creative approaches
for a just and sustainable economy
First Floor, Vine Court, 112-116 Whitechapel Road,
London E1 1JE
T: 0171 377 5696 **F:** 0171 377 5720

New Luddites
Student group that challenges the legitimacy
of science and technology
c/o Green/Yorkleaf, Students Union, Goodricke
College, University of York, York Y01 5DD
e-mail: nedludd@gexpress.gn.apc.org

No Opencast National Support Campaign
Direct action campaigning and networking around
opencast mining
30 Whitehead Close, Earlsfield, SW18 3BT
T: 0171 603 1831

Northwest Pensioners Rights Campaign
Tackles issues such as pensions, the Maastricht
Treaty, VAT on fuel and quangos
64 Leaswood, Skelmersdale, Lancs WN8 6TH
T: 01695 726462

Outrage!
Stages inventive stunts to publicise the struggle
for equal rights for lesbians and gay men
5 Peter Street, London W1 V3RR
T: 0171 439 2381 **F:** 0171 439 3291
e-mail: outrage@cygnet.co.uk
web site: http://OutRage.cygnet.co.uk

Contacts

Permaculture Association
Information and networking on practical ways
of creating ecologically-efficient systems
Chicken Shack Housing Coop, Rhoslefain Tywin,
Gwynedd LL36 9NH
T: 01654 712188

Phreak
Website providing freespace for wierd stuff
e-mail: spiderman@phreak.co.uk
web site: http://www.phreak.co.uk

Ploughshares Support Network
Works to raise British involvement in the international
anti-arms trade Ploughshares movement
which seeks to protect indigenous communities
PO Box X, 111 Magdalen Road, Oxford OX4 1RQ
T: 01603 611953

Positive News
Information about successful ecological and
community activities around the world
6 Bells Pub, Bishops Castle, Shropshire SY9 5AA
T: 01588 630121 **F**: 01588 630122
e-mail: 106074.1577@compuserve.com

Radical Routes
National co-operative providing financial and
other services for housing and workers' co-ops
c/o Cornerstone Housing Coop, 16 Sholebroke
Avenue, Leeds
T/F: 0113 262 9365

Ramblers Association
Campaigns for access to public rights of way and
the open country. Publishes wide range of guides
1-5 Wandsworth Road, London SW8 2XX
T: 0171 582 6878 **F**: 0171 587 3799
e-mail: ramblers@compuserve.com
web site:
http//www.gorp.com/gorp/activity/europe/ra.htm

Reclaim the Streets
Anti-car, anti-capitalism direct action group
PO Box 9656, London N4 4JY
T: 0171 281 4621
e-mail: rts@gn.apc.org

SchNEWS
Weekly newsletter giving information about actions,
and green and civil rights issues. Send first class
stamps or donation to receive copies
c/o Justice?, On the Fiddle, PO Box 2600, Brighton
T: 01273 685913
e-mail: schnews@brighton.co.uk
web site: http://www.clouzz.co.uk/SchNEWS

Slipsteam Organics
Cheltenham home-delivery scheme for organic fruit
and vegetables
34a Langdon Road, Cheltenham, Gloucestershire
T: 01242 680044

Squall
DIY Culture's own quarterly magazine
PO Box 8959, London N19 5HW
T: 0171 561 1204 **F**: 0171 272 9243
e-mail: squall@dircon.co.uk
web site: http://www.phreak.co.uk/squall/

Surfers Against Sewage
Campaigns nationwide for clean seas and helps people
tackle local pollution problems
The Old Counthouse Warehouse, Wheal Kitty, St Agnes,
Cornwall TR5 OPE
T: 01872 553001 **F**: 01872 552615
e-mail: 101450.3353@compuserve.com
web site: http://www.sas.org.uk.

Tepee Valley
Large, long-standing sustainable living settlement
c/o Brig Oubridge, Marchoglwyn Fawr, Llanfynod,
Carmarthen, SA32 7UQ

Tinkers Bubble
Low-impact rural community
Little Norton, Stoke sub Hamden, Somerset TA14
T: 01935 881975

Toxic Alert!
Direct action network focused on the chemical industry
PO Box 2600, Brighton, BN2 2DY
T: 0171 490 0237

Undercurrents
Regular alternative news videos
16B Cherwell Street, Oxford OX4 1BG
T: 01865 203663 **F**: 01865 243562
e-mail: underc@gn.apc.org
web site: http://www.robndina.demon.co.uk/index.htm

United Systems
Networking, advice and information for free parties
c/o Debbie Staunton, 19 Thirleby Road,
Burnt Oak, Middx HA8 OHF
T/F: 0181 959 7525

Urban 75
Central resource website for DIY information
web site: http://194.112.40.4/Urban 75/main.htm

West Devon Environmental Network
Conservation advice, support and information
for local people
c/o Oz Osborne, Bluebells, Brentor, Tavistock,
Devon PL19 OLX
T/F: 01822 810606
e-mail: ozosborne@msn.com

Women Against Pit Closures
National campaign
c/o Silvia Pye, 34 Maple Avenue ,
Newton-le-Willows, Merseyside WA12 8JB
T: 01925 221181

Womens Environmental Network
Informs, educates and empowers women
to protect the environment
87 Worship Street, London EC2A 2BE
T: 0171 247 3327 **F**: 0171 247 4740

Women of the Waterfront
Women's support group for the sacked
Merseyside dockworkers.
See Liverpool Dockers

Photographers

Sarah Chesworth
T: 0171 233 5400

Nick Cobbing
M: 0973 642 103

David Hoffman
T: 0181 981 5041 **F**: 0181 980 2041

Alan Lodge
T/F: 0115 924 5263
e-mail: 100653.3666@compuserve.com
website: http://ourworld.compuserve.com/
homepages/tash_lodge/

Stephen Mayes
T: 0171 252 9601

Alex McNaughton
M: 0374 839660

Adrian Short
T: 0181 641 2867

Alec Smart
M: 0973 559070

Andrew Testa
M: 0973 284607
F: 0171 281 9566
e-mail: testarob@dircon.co,uk.

Photographic Libraries

Manchester Museum of Labour History
103 Princess Street, Manchester M1 6DD
T: 0161 228 7212 **F**: 0161 237 5965

Manchester Central Library
Local Studies Unit, Central Library,
St Peter's Square, Manchester M2 5PD
T: 0161 234 1979 **F**: 0161 234 1963

Illustration

Paul Render
Osbourne House, Barney Lane
Flaxton, York YO6 7RS
T: 01904 468206 **F**: 01904 468613

Design

Jo Shackleton
3 Bickley Howe, Scarborough
East Yorkshire YO12 5TR
F: 01904 468613